FORTRAN to PL/I Dictionary

PL/I to FORTRAN Dictionary

FORTRAN to PL/I
Dictionary

PL/I to FORTRAN
Dictionary

Gary DeWard Brown

A WILEY-INTERSCIENCE PUBLICATION

John Wiley & Sons

New York/London/Sydney/Toronto

Library of Congress Cataloging in Publication Data:

Brown, Gary DeWard.
   FORTRAN to PL/I dictionary, PL/I to FORTRAN
dictionary.

   "A Wiley-interscience publication."
   Includes index.
   1. FORTRAN (Computer program language)—Dictionaries.
2. PL/I (Computer program language)—Dictionaries.
I. Title.

QA76.73.F25B76   001.6'424   74-30147
ISBN 0-471-10796-4

Printed in the United States of America

10 9 8 7 6 5 4 3 2

To Hillary
who dedicated many attentive hours to the manuscript

Preface

Each year, thousands of people must learn a new programming language. With the increasing maturity of the programming field and the expansion of college courses in data processing fundamentals, many of these people may already know another programming language. They are also familiar with the computer, card readers, and computer applications.

This book explains FORTRAN and PL/I in terms of each other, primarily by example, in much the same way in which French is taught in terms of English to someone who speaks English. It is detailed enough so that the reader who is rusty in one of these languages can refresh his memory on its facilities and then proceed to learn the new language through a statement-by-statement comparison. It also serves as a concise reference for both FORTRAN and PL/I. It describes the facilities of each language and illustrates their use.

This book is intended for use in industry, where even experienced programmers must often learn new languages, and in the universities. It can be used both as a text in a structured program where languages are learned in sequence and as a supplementary text for a class in comparative programming languages. The experienced programmer should be able to begin writing in the other language after a quick reading of each section. The student, interested in a more detailed study of the language, should read the book in sequence, performing the exercises to reinforce his knowledge of the language statements.

GARY DeWARD BROWN

August 1974
Los Angeles, California

Contents

FORTRAN to PL/I Dictionary

PL/I to FORTRAN Dictionary

Language Summary

FORTRAN	PL/I	Page

I. GENERAL

CHARACTER SET   19

A to Z
0 to 9
blank = + − * / ( ) , . $

A to Z $ # @
0 to 9
blank = + − * / ( ) , . ' % ; :
¬ & | > < _ ? ‾

STATEMENT FORMAT   19

COMM	STATEMENT NUMBER	CONT	FORTRAN STATEMENT

```
99999  A = B + ( C - D ) / E * F ** G
       Names 1 to 6      Any or no blanks
Label  alphameric        wherever logical
1 to   characters,       for a blank to
99999  first character   appear.
numeric  alphabetic.
         A = 0
         B = 0
```

```
START:  A = B + ( C - D ) / E * F ** G ;
Names and labels         Any or no blanks
1 to 31 alphameric       may appear
characters; first        wherever logical
character alphabetic,    for a blank to
$, #, or @.              appear. Semicolon
                         ends statement.
A, B = 0 ;
```

CONTINUATION   20

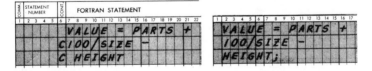

```
VALUE = PARTS +
C100 / SIZE -
C HEIGHT
```

```
VALUE = PARTS +
100 / SIZE -
HEIGHT ;
```

COMMENTS   21

```
C   C IN COL 4.
C   COMMENTS IN COLUMNS
C   1 TO 72.
```

```
/* COMMENTS BETWEEN
DELIMETERS */
/* MAY GO WHERE BLANKS GO */
```

MAIN PROGRAM   86

main program	*program-name*: PROC OPTIONS(MAIN);
STOP	*main program*
END	END *program-name*;

1

HIERARCHY OF OPERATIONS   29

<table>
<tr><td></td><td>Evaluated right to left</td></tr>
<tr><td>Functions</td><td>Functions</td></tr>
<tr><td>A**B</td><td>A**B</td></tr>
<tr><td></td><td>+A −B   (Sign as prefix)</td></tr>
<tr><td></td><td>¬A</td></tr>
</table>

Evaluated left to right

FORTRAN	PL/I
A*B A/B	A*B A/B
A+B A−B	A+B A−B
+A −B (Sign as prefix)	A‖B
A.GT.B etc.	A > B etc.
.NOT.A	
A.AND.B	A&B
A.OR.B	A│B

II. FORTRAN TO PL/I REFERENCE

ASSIGN   30

ASSIGN 500 TO I	DCL I LABEL;
GO TO I,(600,500,400)	I = S500;
	GO TO I;

BACKSPACE   117

BACKSPACE 6

CALL   91

CALL TIME(A,B)	CALL TIME(A,B);

CHARACTER DATA   49

2HAT 4HIT'S 5HME TO   'AT' 'IT''S' 'ME TO'

          or

'AT' 'IT''S' 'ME TO'

No character data type; use integer	DCL *name* CHAR(*length*);
INTEGER A,B	DCL B CHAR(4),
DATA A/4HABCD/	A CHAR(4) INIT('ABCD');

COMMON   76

COMMON A,B(10,20),C(3)	DCL A EXT,
	B(10,20) EXT,
	C(3) EXT;

COMPLEX   42

(3.2,−1.86)	3.2 − 1.86I
COMPLEX A,B	DCL (A,B) COMPLEX FLOAT;
COMPLEX*16 A,B	DCL (A,B) COMPLEX
	FLOAT(16);

CONTINUE

100	CONTINUE	S100: ;

DATA

DATA A/2./,I/3/
INTEGER A/2/,B/3/

DCL A INIT(2E0), I INIT(3);
DCL A FIXED BIN INIT(2),
    B FIXED BIN INIT(3);

LOGICAL
    W/.TRUE./,Y/.FALSE./

DCL W BIT(1) INIT('1'B),
    Y BIT(1) INIT('0'B);

REAL I/2./,J/3./

DCL I FLOAT INIT(2E0),
    J FLOAT INIT(3E0);

REAL*8
    X(3)/2D0,3D0,4D0/

DCL X(3) FLOAT(10)
    INIT(2E0,3E0,4E0);

DEFINE FILE

DEFINE FILE
    file(*max,size*,L,*key*)

DCL FILE(*file-name*) RECORD
    KEYED ENV(REGIONAL(1)
        F(*size*));

DIMENSION

DIMENSION A(10), B(5,2)
INTEGER A(10)
REAL B(5,2)
DOUBLE PRECISION C(20)
    or
REAL*8 C(20)

DCL A(10), B(5,2);
DCL A(10) FIXED BIN;
DCL B(5,2) FLOAT;
DCL C(20) FLOAT(16);

DO

	DO 100 I = 1,10	DO I = 1 TO 10;
100	A(I) = 0.	A(I) = 0;
		END;
	DO 200 I = 1, 10, 2	LOOP: DO I = 1 TO 10 BY 2;
200	A(I) = 0.	A(I) = 0;
		END LOOP;

DOUBLE PRECISION

.10		.10000000000000000E0
D	DOUBLE PRECISION A,B	DCL (A,B) FLOAT DEC(16);
	or	
	REAL*8 A,B	

END

END

END *name*;

FORTRAN	PL/I	Page

<u>END FILE</u> 117

    END FILE 7   CLOSE FILE(F7);

<u>ENTRY</u> 96

    ENTRY FIX(B,C,I);   FIX: ENTRY(B,C,I);

<u>EQUIVALENCE</u> 79

EQUIVALENCE   DCL A,
        (A,B,C),(D,E)   B DEF A,
                          C DEF A,
                          D,
                          E DEF D;

<u>EXTERNAL</u> 95

    EXTERNAL NAME   DCL NAME ENTRY;

<u>FIND</u> 137

    FIND (*file'record*)

<u>FORMAT</u> 121

100	FORMAT(1H1,I6)	S100: FORMAT(PAGE,F(6));
	1H1	PAGE
	1Hb	SKIP
	1H0	SKIP(2)
	1H+	SKIP(0)
	A6	A(6)
	D12.4	E(12,4)
	E12.4	E(12,4)
	F6.2	F(6,2)
	F6.1,F6.1 (Complex)	C(F(6,1),F(6,1)) (Complex)
	G8.2	
	I10	F(10)
	L6	
	'LITERAL' or 7HLITERAL	
	O4 (Octal)	
	2PF6.3	F(6,3,2)
	T6	COL(6)
	X3	X(3)
	Z4 (Hexadecimal)	
	/	SKIP

<u>FUNCTION</u> 87

REAL FUNCTION   DIV: PROC(A,B)
        DIV(A,B)   RETURNS(FLOAT);
DIV = A/B   RETURN(A/B);

RETURN	END DIV;
END	
—	—
C = DIV(W,X)	C = DIV(W,X);

GO TO   29

100	GO TO 200	START: GO TO DONE;
200	GO TO 100	DONE: GO TO START;
		DCL A(3) LABEL
		INIT(S300,S500,S600);
	J = 3	J = 3;
	GO TO (300,500,600),J	GO TO A(J);

IF   31

IF (A.EQ.B) A = 0	IF A = B THEN A = 0;
A.LT.B	A < B
A.GT.B	A > B
A.LE.B	A < = B
A.GE.B	A > = B
A.NE.B	A ⌐ = B
A.GE.B	A ⌐ < B
A.LE.B	A ⌐ > B
A.AND.B	A & B
A.OR.B	A | B
.NOT.A	⌐A
IF (A*B) 400,500,600	IF A*B < 0
	THEN GO TO S400;
	ELSE IF A*B = 0
	THEN GO TO S500;
	ELSE GO TO S600;

IMPLICIT   68

IMPLICIT INTEGER(A,B),	DEFAULT RANGE(A,B)
	FIXED BIN,
REAL(I),	RANGE(I) FLOAT,
REAL(L-W)	RANGE(L:W)
	FLOAT;

INTEGER   40

2 −9 18 0	2 −9 18 0
INTEGER A,B	DCL (A,B) FIXED BIN(31);
INTEGER*2A,B	DCL (A,B) FIXED BIN(15);

LOGICAL   47

.TRUE. .FALSE.	'1'B '0'B
LOGICAL A	DCL A BIT(1);
A = B.GT.C	A = B > C;
IF (A) GO TO 700	IF A THEN GO TO S700;

5

FORTRAN	PL/I	Page
NAMELIST		131

NAMELIST /TA/I,J,K	DCL (TA) FILE;
READ(5,TA)	GET FILE(TA) DATA;
(The data are in the following form)	(The data are in the following form)
bTA I = 6, J = 7, K = 6 &END	I = 6, J = 7, K = 6;
WRITE (6,TA)	PUT FILE(TA) DATA(I.J.K);

PAUSE		141

PAUSE 6	DISPLAY('6');

READ		117

READ (5,100) A,B	GET FILE(FIVE) EDIT (A,B) (R(S100));
100 FORMAT(2F6.3)	S100: FORMAT((2)F(6,3));
	or
	GET FILE(FIVE) EDIT (A,B) ((2)F(6,3));
READ (5,100) (C(I),I = 1,6)	GET FILE(FIVE) EDIT (C(I) DO I = 1 TO 6) (R(S100));
READ (6,100,END = 200, ERR = 300)...	ON ENDFILE(SIX) GO TO S200; ON TRANSMIT(SIX) GO TO S400; GET FILE(SIX) EDIT...
READ (9) A	READ FILE(NINE) INTO (A);
READ (*file'key, fmt*) *data-list*	READ FILE(*file-name*) INTO (*data-list*) KEYFROM(*key*);

REAL		41

2. −9. 18.3 0.22	2E0 −9E0 18.3E0 2.2E−1
or	
2E0 −9E0 18.3E0 2.2E−1	
REAL I,J	DCL (I,J) FLOAT;

RETURN		87

RETURN	RETURN;

REWIND		116

REWIND 5	CLOSE FILE(FIVE);

STOP		87

STOP	RETURN; (In main program) STOP; (In subroutine)

6

SUBROUTINE   90

```
SUBROUTINE TIME(B,I)        TIME: PROC(B,I);
REAL I                         DCL I FLOAT;
RETURN                         RETURN;
END                            END TIME;
        —                              —
CALL TIME(2.,M)             CALL TIME(2E0,M);
```

VARIABLE FORMATS   122

```
READ (5,100) ARRAY
WRITE (10,ARRAY) A,B,C
The FORMAT is data in the
    following form
(2I6,F10.3,A4)
```

WRITE   117

```
WRITE (6,100) D             PUT FILE(SIX) EDIT (D)
                                        (R(S100));
```

```
100    FORMAT(1Hb,F4.0)     S100: FORMAT(SKIP,F(4));
                                        or
                            PUT FILE(SIX) EDIT (D)
                                        (SKIP,F(4));
WRITE (3,300) (C(I), I=1,6) PUT FILE(THREE) EDIT (C(I)
                            DO I=1 TO 6) (R(S300));
WRITE (9) A                 WRITE FILE(NINE)
                                        FROM (A);
WRITE (file'key, fmt) data-list  WRITE FILE(file-name)
                                        FROM (data-list)
                                    KEYFROM(key);
```

III. PL/I TO FORTRAN REFERENCE

ALLOCATE   74

```
ALLOCATE A;
```

ARRAYS   69

```
DCL A(10), B(5,2);          DIMENSION A(10),
                                        B(5,2)
DCL A(10) FIXED BIN;        INTEGER A(10)
DCL B(5,2) FLOAT;           REAL B(5,2)
DCL C(20) FLOAT(16);        DOUBLE
                                PRECISION C(20)
                                        or
                            REAL*8 C(20)

DCL A(1960:1974) FLOAT;
A = 0; (All elements set to zero)
B(2,*) = 0; (Cross-section set to zero)
```

PL/I	FORTRAN	Page

AUTOMATIC
74

DCL A AUTOMATIC; (Core
allocated when procedure invoked)

BEGIN
85

BEGIN;
:
END;

BIT
47

PL/I	FORTRAN
'1'B '0'B	.TRUE. .FALSE.
DCL A BIT(1);	LOGICAL A
A = B > C;	A = B.GT.C
IF A THEN GO TO S700;	IF (A) GO TO 700

BUILTIN
90

DCL SQRT BUILTIN;

CALL
91

CALL TIME(A,B);	CALL TIME(A,B)

DCL SUB ENTRY(FIXED,FLOAT);
CALL SUB(2,6);

CHARACTER DATA
49

'AT' 'IT''S' 'ME TO'	'AT' 'IT''S' 'ME TO'
	or
	2HAT 4HIT'S 5HME TO

DCL (A,B) CHAR(4);	
DCL C CHAR(4) INIT('ABCD');	INTEGER
	C/4HABCD/

A = 'AT';
B = A ‖ 'TO';
DCL J CHAR(200) VAR;

CLOSE
116

CLOSE FILE(F7);	END FILE 7
	or
	REWIND 7
CLOSE FILE(FIVE), FILE(SIX);	END FILE 5
	END FILE 6

COMPILE-TIME STATEMENTS
158

%INCLUDE LIB(*member*);
%DCL A FIXED B CHAR;
%A = 6;
%B = 'CITY';

8

%ACTIVATE A;
%DEACTIVATE A;
%DO I = 1 TO 3;
   ⋮
%END;
%GO TO LABEL;
%LABEL: GO TO START;
%IF I > 4 %THEN %GO TO
                     START;
        %ELSE %A = 4;
%LABEL: PROC;
        ⋮
        %END LABEL;

COMPLEX   42

$3.2 - 1.86I$ $(3.2, - 1.86)$

    DCL (A,B) COMPLEX FLOAT;   COMPLEX A,B
    DCL (A,B) COMPLEX FLOAT(16);   COMPLEX*16 A,B

CONTROLLED   74

    DCL A CTL;
    ALLOCATE A;
    FREE A;

DECLARE   67

    DCL   DATA
                                                INTEGER
                                                REAL
                                                  DOUBLE
                                                          PRECISION
                                                  COMMON
                                                  DIMENSION
                                                  EQUIVALENCE

DEFAULT   68

    DEFAULT RANGE (A,B)   IMPLICIT INTEGER
                 FIXED BINARY,   (A,B),
          RANGE (I) FLOAT,   REAL(I),
          RANGE (L:W) FLOAT;   REAL
                                                  (L-W)

    DEFAULT RANGE (PRO,A,W1)
                 CHAR VALUE(CHAR(2))
                       INIT('XX');
    DEFAULT RANGE (A,B) (10)
                           REAL;

DEFINED   79

    DCL A,   EQUIVALENCE
                                           (A,B,C),(D,E)

```
      B DEF A,
      C DEF A,
      D,
      E DEF D;
  DCL A CHAR(50),
      B CHAR(25) DEF A POS (25);
```

DELAY   171

```
  DELAY(milliseconds);
```

DISPLAY   141

```
  DISPLAY('6');                            PAUSE 6
  DISPLAY('QUESTION')
              REPLY(ANS);
```

DO   33

```
  DO I = 1 TO 10;                          DO 100 I = 1, 10
  A(I) = 0;                      100       A(I) = 0.
  END;
LOOP: DO I = 1 TO 10 BY 2;                 DO 200 I = 1, 10, 2
      A(I) = 0;                  200       A(I) = 0.
      END LOOP;
  DO I = 1, 5, 9;
      —
  DO WHILE (I > 10);
      —
  DO I = 1 TO 10, 12, 15 WHILE
                      (J = K);
      —
  DO;
  :
  END;
```

END   33

```
  END;                                     END
LABEL1: END LABEL2;
```

ENTRY   89

```
FIX: ENTRY(B,C,I);                         ENTRY FIX(B,C,I)
  DCL NAME ENTRY;                          EXTERNAL NAME
```

EXTERNAL   76

```
  DCL A EXT,                               COMMON A,B(10,20),
                                                      C(3)
      B(10,20) EXT,
      C(3) EXT;
```

FILE   116

DCL FILE (F8) RECORD KEYED
    ENV(REGIONAL(1) F(81));
DCL K8 PIC '(8)9';
	DEFINE FILE
	    8(1000,80,L,K8)

FIXED BINARY   40

2 −9 18 0	2 −9 18 0
DCL (A,B) FIXED BIN(31); DCL (C,D) FIXED BIN(15);	INTEGER A,B INTEGER*2 C,D

FIXED DECIMAL   39

2 −3 25 16.4	
DCL A FIXED(6,2);	

FLOAT   41

2E0 −9E0 18.3E0 2.2E−1	2. −9. 18.3 0.22 or 2E0 −9E0 18.3E0 2.2E−1
DCL (I,J) FLOAT;	REAL I,J
.1000000000000000E0	.1D0
DCL (A,B) FLOAT DEC(16);	DOUBLE PRECISION A,B or REAL*8 A,B

FORMAT   121

PL/I		FORTRAN
S100: FORMAT(PAGE,F(6));	100	FORMAT(1H1,I6)
PAGE		1H1
SKIP		1Hb or /
SKIP(2)		1H0
SKIP(0)		1H+
COL(16)		T6
A(6)		A6
B(10)		
C(F(6,1),F(6,1))		F6.1,F6.1
E(12,4)		E12.4 or D12.4
F(10)		I10
F(6,2)		F6.2
F(6,3,2)		2PF6.3
LINE(10)		
P'999V.99'		
X(3)		X3

FREE   74

FREE A;	

FUNCTION   87

PL/I	FORTRAN
DIV: PROC(A,B) RETURNS(FLOAT);	REAL FUNCTION DIV(A,B)
RETURN(A/B); END DIV;	DIV = A/B RETURN END
C = DIV(W,X);	C = DIV(W,X)

GENERIC   96

DCL TIME GENERIC (FTIME
    ENTRY(FLOAT,FLOAT),
DTIME ENTRY(FIXED,FIXED));

GET   117

PL/I		FORTRAN
GET FILE(FIVE) EDIT (A,B) (R(S100));		READ(5,100) A,B
S100: FORMAT((2)F(6,3));	100	FORMAT(2F6.3)
or		
GET FILE(FIVE) EDIT (A,B) ((2)F(6,3));		
GET FILE(FIVE) EDIT (C(I) DO I = 1 TO 6)...		READ (5,100) (C(I), I = 1, 6)
GET FILE(F8) COPY SKIP(2) EDIT...		

GET DATA   131

PL/I	FORTRAN
	NAMELIST /TA/I,J,K READ(5,TA)
GET DATA; (The data are in the following form)	(The data are in the following form)
I=6, J = 7, K=6;	bTA I=6, J = 7, K=6 &END

GET LIST   133

GET FILE(F5) LIST(A,B,C);
(Data are in the following form)
2, 7, 6;

GET STRING   63

GET STRING(*string*) EDIT
   (*variable-list*) (*format-list*);

GO TO   29

PL/I		FORTRAN
START: GO TO DONE;	100	GO TO 200
DONE: GO TO START;	200	GO TO 100
DCL A(3) LABEL INIT(S300,S500, S600);		

PL/I	FORTRAN
J = 3; GO TO A(J);	J = 3 GO TO (300,500,600),J

IF

Page 31

PL/I	FORTRAN

IF A = B THEN A = 0;
IF A > B THEN A = 1.0;
      ELSE A = 0;
A < B
A > B
A < = B
A > = B
A = B
A ¬ = B
A ¬ < B
A ¬ > B
A & B
A | B
¬A
IF A = B THEN DO;
	IF (A.EQ.B) A = 0.
	IF (A.GT.B) A = 1.0
	IF (A.LE.B) A = 0.
	A.LT.B
	A.GT.B
	A.LE.B
	A.GE.B
	A.EQ.B
	A.NE.B
	A.GE.B
	A.LE.B
	A.AND.B
	A.OR.B
	.NOT.A
	IF (A.NE.B)
	      GO TO 100

A = 1;
   B = 2;
   END;   100
	A = 1.
	B = 2.
	CONTINUE

INIT

71

PL/I	FORTRAN
DCL A INIT(2E0), I INIT(3);	DATA A/2./,I/3/
DCL A FIXED BIN INIT(2), B FIXED BIN INIT(3);	INTEGER A/2/,B/3/
DCL W BIT(1) INIT('1'B),	LOGICAL W/.TRUE./,Y/.FALSE./
Y BIT(1) INIT('0'B);	
DCL A FLOAT INIT(2E0), B FLOAT INIT(3E0);	REAL I/2./,J/3./

DCL X(3) FLOAT(16) INIT(2E0,
        3E0,4E0);
	REAL*8 X(3)/2D0,
	      3D0,4D0/

DCL M CHAR(3) INIT('XYZ');	

LIST PROCESSING

163

```
DCL A BASED(B) CHAR(10);
ALLOCATE A;
FREE A;
DCL D POINTER;
ALLOCATE A SET D;
D– >A = 'THIS';
READ (F9) SET(B);
LOCATE B FILE(F9);
```

LOCATE

    LOCATE A FILE(F9);

S100: ;   100   CONTINUE

    ON CONV (CONVERSION)
    ON ENDFILE(*file*)   READ(*file*,*fmt*,
                                                           END = *label*)
    ON ENDPAGE(*file*)
    ON ERROR
    ON FINISH
    ON FOFL (FIXEDOVERFLOW)   CALL OVERFLOW(I)
    ON NAME(*file*)
    ON OFL (OVERFLOW)   CALL OVERFLOW(I)
    ON RECORD(*file*)
    ON SIZE
    ON STRG (STRINGRANGE)
    ON STRZ (STRINGSIZE)
    ON SUBRG (SUBSCRIPTRANGE)
    ON TRANSMIT(*file*)   READ(*file*,*fmt*,
                                                           ERR = *label*)
    ON UNDF(*file*) (UNDEFINEDFILE)
    ON UFL (UNDERFLOW)   CALL OVERFLOW(I)
    ON ZDIV (ZERODIVIDE)   CALL DVCHCK(I)

    OPEN FILE(A) INPUT, FILE(B)
                 OUTPUT;   First read or write opens file.
    OPEN FILE(F6) PRINT
        LINESIZE(132) PAGESIZE(66);

    DCL A PIC '(4)Z9V99';
        9   Decimal digit
        V   Decimal alignment
        Z   Leading zero suppress
        Y   Zero suppress
        .   Decimal point
        ,   Comma
        /   Slash
        B   Blank
        $ Dollar sign
        S   Sign
        −   Minus sign
        +   Plus sign

CR   Credit
DB   Debit

PUT   117

PUT FILE(SIX) EDIT (D)	WRITE (6,100) D
(R(S100));	
S100: FORMAT(SKIP,F(4)); 100	FORMAT(1Hb,F4.0)
or	
PUT FILE(SIX) EDIT (D)	
(SKIP,F(4));	
PUT FILE(THREE) EDIT (C(I) DO	WRITE (3,300) (C(I),
I = 1 TO 6);	I = 1, 6)

PUT FILE(SIX) EDIT PAGE
     SKIP(2) LINE(10) (E) (F(10,2));

PUT DATA   117

PUT DATA(I,J,K);	NAMELIST /TA/ I,J,K
	WRITE (6,TA)

PUT LIST   117

PUT FILE(F6) LIST(A,B,C);

PUT STRING   63

PUT STRING(*string*) EDIT
     (*variable-list*) (*format-list*);

READ   130

READ FILE(NINE) INTO (A);	READ (9) A
READ FILE(F8) INTO (A)	READ (8'KEY,100) A
KEYFROM(KEY); 100	FORMAT(A10)

RECURSIVE   173

N2: PROC(N) RECURSIVE
     RETURNS(FIXED);

REGIONAL   135

DCL FILE(F8) RECORD KEYED	DEFINE FILE 8(1000,
ENV(REGIONAL(1) F(81));	80,L,K8)

RETURN   87

RETURN;	RETURN
	(in subroutine)
	STOP
	(in main program)

RETURN(*function-value*);

Chapter 1

Introduction

This book is not a conventional programming text. Most programming manuals are written for the beginner, who is assumed not to know another programming language. But the programming profession has matured; today many people learning a new programming language already know another programming language. One who knows English and is learning French need not learn what a mushroom is, for example, but only that the French word for mushroom is *champignon*. In the same way, one already familiar with a programming language need not learn the meaning of an array, but only the language statements required to define and manipulate arrays.

I. PURPOSE OF THIS BOOK

This book is intended for the person who knows FORTRAN or PL/I and who wants to learn PL/I or FORTRAN. The book compares the two languages in detail and serves as a handy reference text for both FORTRAN and PL/I. For those impatient to learn FORTRAN or PL/I by building upon knowledge that they already have, this book skips computer history, applications, and programming fundamentals and goes directly to the FORTRAN and PL/I statements.

II. SCOPE OF THIS BOOK

All of ANS FORTRAN as well as most of the widely used non-ANS FORTRAN IV features are described, including those of the WATFOR and WATFIV Waterloo FORTRAN compilers. The book examines IBM's Version Five, Level F PL/I implementation, because its frequent use makes it a de facto standard. The volume covers all of PL/I that is related to FORTRAN, and gives a brief overview of those features not related to FORTRAN. The additional features of the IBM Checkout and Optimizing compilers are also included.

III. THE LANGUAGES

FORTRAN, an acronym derived from FORmula TRANslator, was the first widely used high-level programming language. Today it is still perhaps the most widely known programming language. FORTRAN compilers exist on almost all general-purpose computers. FORTRAN is a relatively simple, efficient, easy-to-learn, mathematically oriented language intended primarily for scientific applications in the manipulation of numeric data.

PL/I, an acronym derived from Programming Language/One, is younger than FORTRAN. PL/I was developed to serve both scientific and business applications. It was created jointly by IBM and representatives of two organizations—SHARE, a scientific users' group, and GUIDE, its commercial counterpart. Until recently, PL/I availability has been limited mainly to IBM computers, but now other manufacturers have begun to introduce PL/I compilers.

PL/I has many more features than FORTRAN, but it pays a price for this in efficiency. PL/I programs generally take slightly longer to compile, require more core storage, and consume more execution time than do comparable FORTRAN programs. However, many applications either are easier to write in PL/I than in FORTRAN or are not possible at all in FORTRAN. Statement for statement, PL/I is as easy to learn as FORTRAN, but there is much more to learn, since PL/I is more extensive.

IV. FORMAT OF THIS BOOK

The language features of FORTRAN and PL/I are organized into chapters. The use of each statement is described and coding examples are given. The comparable statements are placed side by side down the page with FORTRAN on the left and PL/I on the right, so that the statements of the one language are also explained in terms of the other. Language statements are written in uppercase letters; lowercase italic type denotes generic terms, such as *name* or *value*.

V. USE OF THIS BOOK

When used as a textbook, the chapters should be read in sequence and the exercises performed at the end of each chapter. The experienced programmer, however, may wish to choose selected chapters. The "Language Summary" at the beginning illustrates the features of both FORTRAN and PL/I and cites the pages where the features are described in more detail. The book is intended to be used in much the same way in which an English/French dictionary would be used to look up words (language statements in this case) to translate from one language to the other.

Chapter 2

General Rules

FORTRAN

I. CHARACTER SET

A through Z are alphabetic.

0 through 9 are numeric.

b† = + − * / ( ) , . $ are special; particular implementations may allow other characters.

PL/I

A through Z, $, #, and @ are alphabetic.

0 through 9 are numeric.

b† = + − * / ( ) , . ' % ; : ¬ & | > < _ ? are special. PL/I programs can also be written using a 48-character set as described in Appendix A.

II. STATEMENT FORMAT

A. General Format

FORTRAN is oriented toward punched cards with one statement per line.

There is no statement delimiter because a line delimits a statement.

Columns 1 to 5 contain statement labels, a C punched in column 6 denotes a continued line, and columns 7 to 72 contain the statement. Columns 73 to 80 are available for sequencing the card deck.

PL/I statements are considered to be a continuous stream of characters with part, a whole, or several statements per line.

A semicolon (;) delimits a statement.

Statements are normally coded in columns 2 to 72 for card input, although the installation can specify other columns. A line can contain both statements and statement labels. Columns 73 to 80 are then available for sequencing the card deck.

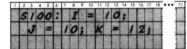

The WATFIV dialect of FORTRAN permits all FORTRAN statements except the FORMAT statement to optionally be written similar to PL/I statements with several statements per card, each delimited by a semicolon. Statements labels, as described below for PL/I, are followed by a colon.

† The lowercase b is used to represent a blank character.

FORTRAN	PL/I

B. Continuation of Statements

If a statement exceeds one line, continue the statement onto the next line by coding a C in column 6 of each continued line. (Any non-blank, nonzero character will do.)

If a statement exceeds one line, continue the statement onto the next line. The delimeter eliminates the need to mark the continuation.

C. Blanks within Statements

In general, blanks have no meaning unless used as data. One may use any or no blanks wherever it is reasonable or appropriate to code a blank.

$$A = 1.3 + FIVE$$
$$A = \quad 1.3 + FIVE$$

$$A = 1.3 + FIVE;$$
$$A = \quad 1.3 + FIVE;$$

III. STATEMENT LABELS

Statement labels have values 1 to 99999, and are written in columns 1 to 5. The value of the label has no meaning; labels need not be consecutive or ascending, although programs are much easier to read if they are.

Statement labels are 1 to 31 alphanumeric (A–Z, \$, #, @, 0 to 9) or break (_) characters. The first character must be alphabetic (A–Z, \$, #, @), and the label is followed by a colon (:). Labels precede statements, but need not be in any particular columns, or even on the same line.

```
100        GO TO 200
200        IF (I.EQ.0) GO TO 100
```

```
START_IT: GO TO NEXT;
NEXT:
          IF I=0 THEN GO TO START_IT;
```

IV. VARIABLE NAMES

Names are 1 to 6 alphanumeric (A–Z, 0–9) characters. The first character must be alphabetic (A–Z).

The same rules apply to names as apply to statement labels. Names are 1 to 31 alphanumeric (A–Z, \$, #, @, 0–9) or break (_) characters. The first character must be alphabetic (A–Z, \$, #, @).

FORTRAN	PL/I

X FIVE STORES STETAX

Variables with names beginning I to N default to integer; the same as PL/I binary fixed-point with precision (31,0).

X FIVE STORES STATE_TAX

Variables with names beginning I to N default to binary fixed-point with precision (15,0); the same as FORTRAN half-word integer.

I NAME KEY

Variables with names beginning A to H and O to Z default to single-precision full-word real; the same as PL/I decimal floating-point with six decimal digits of precision.

I NAME KEY_TO_LOCK

Variables with names beginning A to H, O to Z, $, #, and @ default to decimal floating-point with six decimal digits of precision; the same as FORTRAN single-precision full-word real.

Z TIME SIZE

Z TIME SIZE

V. COMMENTS

Comments are written one per card by coding a "C" in column 1 and the comment in columns 2 to 72.

C THIS IS A COMMENT.

Comments may be written wherever a blank can appear. Comments begin with /* and end with */.

/* THIS IS A COMMENT. */
A/*HERE*/ = /*HERE*/ 12;
                    /*OR HERE*/

Two errors are common with PL/I comments. First, the */ to end the comment may be forgotten. The compiler ends the comment with the next */ it encounters; usually the */ terminating the next comment, and any intervening statements are treated as comments. The second error results from the IBM System/360/370 implementation in which a /* in columns 1 and 2 is a system control card signaling the end of the input stream. If a comment begins in column 1, the remainder of the program is skipped. (PL/I statements usually begin in column 2 rather than column 1 for this reason.)

VI. ABBREVIATIONS

FORTRAN has no abbreviations.

Most long PL/I key words can be abbreviated; DCL for DECLARE, DEC for DECIMAL, etc. This dictionary generally uses the abbreviation rather than the long form. Appendix B lists PL/I abbreviations.

VII. RESERVED WORDS

No reserved words exist in either FORTRAN or PL/I. (There is an exception in the 48-character set PL/I. The special words described in Appendix A are reserved in the 48-character set PL/I.) The compilers can always distinguish statement names from variable names by the context in which they are used. As a result, there is no conflict in using statement names as variable names.

IF (IF.EQ.3) DO = 6.0   IF IF = 3 THEN DO = 6.0;

VIII. PSEUDOVARIABLES

PL/I has *pseudovariables*, which are built-in functions that can appear on the left-hand side of the assignment statement. For example, the IMAG function on the right-hand side of the assignment statement (I = IMAG(Y);) is a normal function that returns the imaginary part of a complex number. The IMAG function on the left-hand side of the assignment statement (IMAG(Y) = I;) is a pseudovariable that stores the value on the right-hand side of the assignment statement into the imaginary part of the complex number Y on the left-hand side.

IX. PROGRAM ORGANIZATION

FORTRAN and PL/I both have main programs, and execution begins with the first executable statement in the main program. Execution continues in sequence unless altered by other statements. Both FORTRAN and PL/I have external subroutines that are invoked by the CALL statement, and external functions that return a single value. PL/I has in addition internal functions and subroutines; FORTRAN has internal one-statement functions.

PL/I can group several statements between a DO; and END; pair to be executed in sequence wherever a single statement would normally appear, as for example in the IF statement. Such a grouping of statements is called a *DO-group*.

	IF (A.NE.B) GO TO 100	IF A = B THEN DO;
	C = D	C = D;
	E = F	E = F;
100	CONTINUE	END;

PL/I can also group statements between a BEGIN; and END; pair. The BEGIN/END pair, called a *begin block*, is similar to the DO-group, but limits the scope of names and can allocate dynamic storage. The final grouping of statements are enclosed between a PROC; and END; pair. Such a group is called a *procedure block*, and constitutes an internal subroutine. The procedure is similar to a block, but it can only be invoked by the CALL statement. The flow of control passes around the procedure, whereas it passes through the block and DO-group. Program organization is described in more detail in Chapter 8.

Statements must appear in the following order within a program.

1. Job card and system control statements.
2. Any IMPLICIT statement.

1. Job card and system control statements.
2. *procedure-name*: PROC OPTIONS
   (MAIN);

FORTRAN	PL/I
IMPLICIT INTEGER(A,B)	COMP: PROC OPTIONS (MAIN);

3. DIMENSION, DATA, Type, EQUIVALENCE, COMMON, DOUBLE PRECISION, and EXTERNAL statements. (May go anywhere, but usually placed here.)

3. DCL statements to define files and names (May go anywhere, but usually placed here.)

FORTRAN	PL/I
DIMENSION AX(10),IX(20)	DCL AX(10),IX(20);
DATA I/1/,A/20./	DCL I INIT(1), A INIT(20E0);
INTEGER AT,OF	DCL (AT,OF) FIXED BIN(31);
EQUIVALENCE (I,B)	DCL B DEF I;
COMMON X,Y	DCL (X,Y) EXT;
DOUBLE PRECISION BIG, HUGE	DCL (BIG,HUGE) FLOAT(16);
EXTERNAL SUB1,SUB2	DCL (SUB1,SUB2) ENTRY; DCL (IN,OUT) FILE;

4. Program statements of the main body.

4. Program statements of the main body.

```
FORTRAN                                PL/I

50    READ (5,100,END=800) D,N          ON ENDFILE(IN) GO TO
                                                          DONE;
100   FORMAT(F5.2,I3)                   START: GET FILE(IN) EDIT (D,N)
                                                      (F(5,2),F(3));
      WRITE (6,110) D,N                 PUT FILE(OUT) EDIT
                                                          (D,N)
110   FORMAT(1H ,F5.2,I3)                 (SKIP,F(5,2),F(3));
      DO 120 I = 1,10                     DO I = 1 TO 10;
120   A = (A*B)/((C−D)**3)                A = (A*B)/((C−D)**3);
                                          END;
      IF (A.EQ.B) A = 0.              IF A = B THEN A = 0E0;
      IF (A.NE.B) A = A + B                ELSE A = A + B;
      CALL SUB3(X,Y)                   CALL SUB3(X,Y);
      GO TO 50                          GO TO START;
800   CONTINUE                         DONE:
        ⋮                                 ⋮
```

5. Statement to stop execution.

5. Statement to stop execution. (Execution also stops if the last END statement is executed.)

FORTRAN	PL/I
STOP	RETURN;

6. Program termination statement. (Does not stop program execution.)
   END

6. Program termination statement. (Also stops program execution if executed.)
   label: END *procedure-name*;
   FINISH: END COMP;

7. Any subroutines or functions.

   SUBROUTINE *name(a,b,c,...)*
   Statements within subroutine.

7. Any subroutines or functions.

   name: PROC(*a,b,c,...*);
   Statements within subroutine.

23

FORTRAN	PL/I
RETURN	RETURN;
Possibly more statements.	*Possibly more statements.*
END	*label*: END *name*;
FUNCTION *name(a,b,c,...)*	*name*: PROC*(a,b,c,...)*;
Statements within function.	*Statements within function.*
name = value	RETURN*(value)*;
RETURN	
Possibly more statements.	*Possibly more statements.*
END	*label*: END *name*;

8. Any system control statements, data, etc.

8. Any system control statements, data, etc.

X.   EXERCISES

1. Tell which of the following data names are incorrect, and why.

FORMULA	FORMULA
TEXT	TEXT
STOP_AT	STOP_AT
2HOT	2HOT
F-111	F-111
H24	H24
HUT_16	HUT_16
OH**	OH**
A	A
MEET_ME@4	MEET_ME@4
UP TO	UP TO
NOT-HERE	NOT-HERE

2. Tell which of the following statement labels are incorrect, and why.

100	100:
1	1:
10.7	NOW
1,000	HERE:
100000	TO_HERE:
1 1	HERE: AND_HERE:
4725	EITHER/OR:
	ALL DONE:
	FINISH;

3. Write the minimum number of statements required for a main program, a subroutine, and a function.

4. List all of the errors in the following program.

C MAIN PROGRAM		/* MAIN PROGRAM	
100	A = 100**2 − 7.6	100:	A = 100**2 − 7.6
	+ 3.4		+ 3.4;
50	B = A/2.0	S50:	B = A/2.0
	IF(B.EQ.0)GOTO200		IF(B=0)THENGOTODONE;
	C = A*B C FIND A*B.		C = A*B /*FIND A*B*/;
	GO TO 50		GO TO S50;
200	A = 0		DONE A = 0;
	END		END;

5. Discuss the relative advantages and disadvantages of the one statement per line concept of FORTRAN versus the statement delimeter concept of PL/I.

Chapter 3

Basic Language Statements

FORTRAN   PL/I

I. NULL STATEMENT

The null statement can appear wherever an executable statement can appear, and has no effect on processing.

The CONTINUE statement is the null statement, and usually has a label.

The semicolon (;) is the null statement, and may have a label.

100	CONTINUE

S100: ;

The CONTINUE statement is used to terminate DO loops that otherwise might end with an IF, GO TO, RETURN, STOP, or PAUSE statement.

The null statement is used to return control from an ON unit (described in Chapter 11) without executing any instructions.

The CONTINUE statement is also used to insert a label in a program without disturbing other statements.

Labels need not be on the same line as statements, and can be inserted freely.

200	CONTINUE

S200:

II. ASSIGNMENT STATEMENT

The assignment statement assigns to the variable on the left the value of the expression on the right.

$$A = 6$$ $$A = 6;$$

There can be only a single variable on the left.

There can be several variables on the left separated by commas, and each is assigned the value of the expression on the right.

$$N = 0$$
$$J = 0$$

$$N, J = 0;$$

The WATFOR and WATFIV FORTRAN compilers permit several variables separated by equal signs to be assigned a single value in assignment statement.

$$N = J = 0$$ $$N, J = 0;$$

III. OPERATIONS

A. Arithmetic Operations

FORTRAN		PL/I	
+	Add	+	Add
−	Subtract	−	Subtract
*	Multiply	*	Multiply
/	Divide	/	Divide
**	Exponential	**	Exponential

$$X = (A + (B - C)$$
$$*D/E)**2$$

$$X = (A + (B - C)$$
$$*D/E)**2;$$

B. Relational Operations

FORTRAN		PL/I	
.LT.	Less than	<	Less than
.GT.	Greater than	>	Greater than
.LE.	Less than or equal	<=	Less than or equal
.GE.	Greater than or equal	>=	Greater than or equal
.EQ.	Equal	=	Equal
.NE.	Not equal	¬=	Not equal
.GE.	Greater than or equal	¬<	Not less than
.LE.	Less than or equal	¬>	Not greater than

          IF (A.GT.B) GO TO 100   IF A > B THEN GO TO S100;

C. Logical Operations

.AND. Logical And. If A and B are both true, then A.AND.B has the value true; if either A or B or both are false, then A.AND.B has the value false.

& Logical And. If A and B are both true (value of '1'B), then A & B has the value of true; if either A or B or both are false (value of '0'B), then A & B has the value false. (PL/I uses bit-strings consisting of the binary digits 1 and 0 in place of logical data. The 1 represents true and 0 false.)

.OR. Logical Or. If either A or B or both are true, then A.OR.B has the value true; if both A and B are false, then A.OR.B has the value false.

| Logical Or. If either A or B or both are true, then A | B has the value true; if both A and B are false, then A | B has the value false.

.NOT. Logical Not. If A is true, then .NOT.A has the value false; if A is false, then .NOT.A has the value true.

¬ Logical Not. If A is true, then ¬A has the value false; if A is false, then ¬A has the value true.

D. Bit-String Operations

Not in FORTRAN.

The logical operations, (&, |, and ¬) can be applied to entire bit-strings.

          '011010'B&'101100'B yields '001000'B
          '011010'B|'101100'B yields '111110'B
          ¬'011010'B yields '100101'B

E. Character-String Operations

Not in FORTRAN.

‖ Concatenation. The character-string on the right is appended to the end of the character-string on the left.

'ABC'‖'DEF' yields 'ABCDEF'

F. Hierarchy of Operations

The hierarchy listed below specifies the order, from highest to lowest, in which operations are performed. The hierarchy can be overridden by parentheses, with the operations in the inner-most parentheses being performed first. It is good practice to use parentheses, because the hierarchy is apparent when they are used.

- Evaluation of functions (SQRT, etc.)
- Exponential (A**B)

The above are usually evaluated from right to left when operations have equal hierarchy, but some compilers evaluate them from left to right. Use parentheses if you are at all uncertain.

2**3**4 is usually evaluated as 2**(3**4)

- Evaluation of functions (SQRT, etc.)
- Exponential (A**B)
- Sign as prefix (+A −B)
- Logical Not (—A)

The above are evaluated from right to left when operations have equal hierarchy.

2**3**4 is evaluated as 2**(3**4)

The operations below are evaluated from left to right when the operations have equal hierarchy.

- Multiply, Divide (A*B/C)
- Add, Subtract (A+B−C)

- Relational Operations (A.GT.B)
- Logical Not (.NOT.A)
- Logical And (A.AND.B)
- Logical Or (A.OR.B)

No two arithmetic operations may appear consecutively. Y = X**−2 must be coded as Y = X**(−2).

- Multiply, Divide (A*B/C)
- Add, Subtract (A+B−C)
- Concatenation (A ‖ B)
- Relational Operations (A > B)

- Logical And (A&B)
- Logical Or (A | B)

Arithmetic operations may appear con-secutively as in Y = X**−2;

IV. CONTROL STATEMENTS

A. GO TO Statements

The GO TO statement transfers control to another labeled statement.

FORTRAN	PL/I

| 100   GO TO 200 | START: GO TO END_IT_ALL; |
| 200   GO TO 100 | END_IT_ALL: GO TO START; |

B. Multiple GO TO Statement

The multiple GO TO statements allow a transfer to one of several labels, depending on the contents of a variable.

Labels are assigned to integer variables by the ASSIGN statement. The GO TO must then name all labels that can be assigned to the variable.

```
            ASSIGN 500 TO I
            GO TO I,(400,500,600)
                (Same as GO TO 500)
```

The ASSIGN statement can only assign labels listed in the GO TO statement.

```
            ASSIGN 400 TO I
            GO TO I,(400,500,600)
                (Same as GO TO 400)
```

The computed GO TO allows the GO TO to be based upon the value of an integer variable. The variable can have positive values of 1 to n where n is the number of labels listed in the GO TO statement. A value of 1 causes a transfer to the first label in the list, a value of 2 to the second, etc.

```
            J = 3
            GO TO (300,500,600),J
                (Same as GO TO 600)
```

Labels can be treated as data and assigned to variables that are declared LABEL by the DCL statement. The GO TO statement names the variable, and the transfer is made to the label assigned to the variable.

```
            DCL I LABEL;
            I = S500;
            GO TO I;
                (Same as GO TO S500;)
```

Once a variable is declared to be a label variable, it can be assigned any label.

```
            I = S400;
            GO TO I;
                (Same as GO TO S400;)
```

Label variables can also be declared as arrays, and can be assigned initial values.

```
            DCL WHERE(3) LABEL INIT(S300,
                                    S500,S600);
            J = 3;
            GO TO WHERE(J);
                (Same as GO TO S600;)
```

Subscripted names of a label array can be used as labels, obviating the need to initialize the label array.

```
            DCL SEND(3) LABEL;
                :
            SEND(1): A = B + C;
                :
            SEND(2): A = B - C;
                :
            SEND(3): A = B/C;
                :
```

J = 2;
GO TO SEND(J);
        (Same as GO TO SEND(2);)

C. IF Statement

The IF statement allows statements to be executed depending on a conditional test. The general form of the IF statement is as follows:

IF *(condition) statement*

      IF *condition* THEN *statement*;
        ELSE *statement*;

The *condition* is any relational expression or logical variable. The *statement* is executed if the *condition* is true. If the *condition* is false, the *statement* is skipped. The *statement* can be any executable statement except a DO or another logical IF statement.

The *condition* is any relational expression or a bit-string. The THEN *statement* is executed if the *condition* is true (or any bit in a bit-string is equal to 1), and the ELSE *statement* is executed if the *condition* is false (or all bits in a bit-string are equal to zero).

IF (A.GT.B) A = 1.0

IF (A.LE.B) A = 0.

      IF A $>$ B THEN A = 1.0;
        ELSE A = 0.;

The ELSE portion of the IF statement is optional, and if omitted, execution continues with the statement following.

IF (A.EQ.B) GO TO 200

IF A = B THEN GO TO S200;

IF statements cannot be nested.

IF statements can be nested to any level.

IF (A.LE.B) GO TO 300

IF (X.EQ.Y) A = 0.

IF (X.NE.Y) A = 1.0
GO TO 400
300   IF (X.GT.Y) A = $-$1.0
        IF (X.LE.Y) A = $-$2.0
400   CONTINUE

      IF A $>$ B THEN IF X$=$Y
          THEN A$=$0; ELSE A$=$1;
      ELSE IF X $>$ Y THEN
          A$=-$1; ELSE A$=-$2;

The statement above is better understood if it is written indented in the manner in which it is executed. Always indent the IF statement to show the logical sequence.

IF A $>$ B
   THEN IF X = Y
      THEN A = 0;
      ELSE A = 1;
   ELSE IF X $>$ Y
      THEN A = $-$1;
      ELSE A = $-$2:

Each ELSE clause is always associated with the innermost unmatched IF. An ELSE with a null statement may be required to give the desired result. In the following example, the first 'ELSE;' is required to pair the 'ELSE IF A = C' clause with the proper 'THEN' clause. The final 'ELSE;' could have been omitted.

```
        IF (A.LE.C) GO TO 500
        IF (B.LT.D) A = A + 1.0
        GO TO 600
500     IF (A.EQ.C) A = A + 2.0
600     CONTINUE
```

```
IF A > C
    THEN IF B < D
            THEN A = A + 1;
            ELSE;
    ELSE IF A = C
            THEN A = A + 2;
            ELSE;
```

The IF statement can execute only one statement.

The IF statement can execute several statements by enclosing the statements between a DO; and END; pair termed a DO group. (See Chapter 8 for a full description of the DO; END; pair.)

```
        IF (A*B/C.LE.D) GO TO 100
        A = 100.0
        B = 200.0
        GO TO 200
100     A = 1.0
        B = 2.0
        C = 3.0
200     CONTINUE
```

```
IF A*B/C > D
    THEN DO; A = 100;
            B = 200;
            END;
    ELSE  DO; A = 1;
            B = 2;
            C = 3;
            END;
```

The IF statement can test logical variables.

Logical variables are represented by a bit-string of length 1. A value of '1'B is true, and '0'B is false.

```
        LOGICAL A
        A = B.GT.C
        IF (A) GO TO 700
```

```
DCL A BIT(1);
A = B > C;
IF A THEN GO TO S700;
```

FORTRAN has a three-way arithmetic IF statement. A transfer is made to one of three labels, depending on whether the expression is less than 0 (first label), equal to 0 (second label), or greater than 0 (third label). The general form is as shown.

> IF *(expression) label,label,*
>   *label*
>   <0   =0   >0
> IF (A*B) 400,500,600

> IF A*B<0
>   THEN GO TO S400;
>   ELSE IF A*B = 0
>   THEN GO TO S500;
>   ELSE GO TO S600;

D.   DO Statement

The DO statement allows statements within its range (a DO *loop*) to be executed repeatedly with a control variable *i* assigned values from *m1* to *m2* by steps of *m3*.

> DO *label i = m1, m2, m3*

> *label* statement

> *label*: DO *i = m1* TO *m2* BY *m3*;

> END *label*;

The DO loop can end with any executable statement except a GO TO, IF, STOP, RETURN, PAUSE, or DO. DO loops can be terminated with the null CONTINUE statement if they would otherwise terminate with a GO TO, IF, STOP, RETURN, or PAUSE.

The DO loop ends with an END statement that may, optionally, give the label of the DO statement.

> DO 100 I = 1, 10, 2
> IF (A(I).EQ.B) GO TO 200
>
> 100   CONTINUE

> TIMES: DO I = 1 TO 10 BY 2;
>   IF A(I) = B THEN GO TO
>   DATE;
>   END TIMES;

If the label is omitted after the END statement, it is assumed to refer to the previous DO.

> DO I = 1 TO 10 BY 2;
> IF A(I) = B THEN GO TO DATE;
> END;

The control variable *i* must be an integer variable.

The control variable *i* may be any variable.

m1, *m2*, and *m3* must be integer variables or constants.

m1, *m2*, and *m3* may be variables, constants, or expressions.

m3 must be greater than zero.

m3 may be positive or negative. If negative, *i* is decremented by *m3* until *i* < *m2*.

> DO I = 100 TO 1 BY −1;

FORTRAN	PL/I

m3 is assumed to be equal to 1 if it is omitted.

    DO 100 I = 3, 10 is equivalent to
    DO 100 I = 3, 10, 1

The test for $i > m2$ is made at the end of the loop. Hence the loop is always executed at least once. In the statement DO 100 I = J, 10, the loop is executed once if J is equal to 11.

The control variable i has no predictable value at the end of a loop.

m3 is assumed to be equal to 1 if it is omitted.

    DO I = 3 TO 10; is equivalent to
    DO I = 3 TO 10 BY 1;

The test for $i > m2$ (or $i < m2$ if *m3* is negative) is made at the start of the loop, and the loop is not executed if *m1* > *m2* (or *m1* < *m2* if *m3* is negative). In the statement DO I = J TO 10; the loop is not executed if J is equal to 11.

The control variable i contains the next value greater than *m2* (or less than *m2* if *m3* is negative) at the end of the loop. In the statement DO I = 1 TO 11 BY 3; I would equal 14 at the end of the loop.

If a branch is made out of a loop, the control variable i contains its current value. A branch cannot be made into the middle of a DO loop. Nor may the control variable i be changed within the loop. DO statements can be nested to any level.

```
        DO 500 I = 1, 10              DO I = 1 TO 10;
        A = A + 1.0                   A = A + 1.0;
        DO 400 J = 1, 20              DO J = 1 TO 20;
        B = B + 1.0                   B = B + 1.0;
400     CONTINUE                      END;
        C = C + 1.0                   C = C + 1.0;
        D = D + 1.0                   D = D + 1.0;
500     CONTINUE                      END;
```

Several nested DO loops may terminate on the same statement.

A single labeled END statement terminates all inner DO loops.

```
600     DO 700 I = 1, 10          S600: DO I = 1 TO 10;
        DO 700 J = 1, 20                DO J = 1 TO 20;
700     A(I,J) = 0.                     A(I,J) = 0.0;
                                        END S600;
```

The DO can name specific values for the control variable i with the form DO $i = v1$, $v2$, $v3$,...; The statement DO I = 7, −3, 6; repeats the loop for I = 7, −3, and 6. This form of the DO loop can be combined with the *m1* TO *m2* BY *m3* form. In the following example, the loop is repeated for I = 4, 15, 6, 1, 2, 3, 7, 9, 11, and 12.

    DO I = 4, 15, 6, 1 TO 3, 7 TO 11 BY 2,
                           12;

FORTRAN   PL/I

A loop can be repeated while a condition is true. The form is DO WHILE (*condition*);. In the following example, the loop is executed four times.

	FORTRAN	PL/I
	A = −4.0	A = −4.0;
800	IF (A.GE.0.) GO TO 900	DO WHILE (A < 0.);
	A = A + 1.0	A = A + 1.0;
	GO TO 800	END;
900	CONTINUE	

The WHILE clause can be combined with the other forms of the DO loop.

	FORTRAN	PL/I
	DO 910 I = 1, 10	DO I = 1 TO 10 WHILE (X > B);
	IF (X.LE.B) GO TO 920	X = X + Y(I);
910	X = X + Y(I)	END;
920	CONTINUE	

V. EXERCISES

1. What will the variables A and B contain after the following statements have been executed?

FORTRAN	PL/I
A = 1.	A, B = 1;
B = A + 1.	B, A = A + 1;
A = A + B	A, B = A + B;

2. Place parentheses around the following statements to indicate the hierarchy of operations.

A**B−2/Y−D	A**B−2/Y−D
A+2*C**2/B+6*4	A+2*C**2/B+6*4
A+B.EQ.0.OR.A.NE.1.0. AND.B.GT.A	A+B=0|A¬=1.0&B>A

3. The following table contains statement labels and associated values of the variable I. Branch to the proper statement label as given by the value of I using first the IF statement and then a multiple GO TO statement.

I	Label		I	Label
1	600		1	S600
2	400		2	S400
3	150		3	S150
4	1000		4	S1000

4. Use IF statements to set the variable J to the appropriate value based on the conditions given.

Value of J	Condition
0	If A equals zero.
−1	If A is negative and B is not greater than zero.
−2	If A and B + C are greater than 22.
100	If A equals 1 or B equals 1 or half of B + C equals 1.

5. What values will I assume within the following loops?

(a)

```
      DO 100 I = −10,21,3          DO I = −10 TO 21 BY 3;
      A(I) = 0.                    A(I) = 0;
100   CONTINUE                     END;
```

(b)

```
      DO 200 I = 1,1               DO I = 1 TO 1;
      A(I) = 0.                    A(I) = 0;
200   CONTINUE                     END;
```

(c)

```
                                   DO I = −3 TO −7 BY −2, 8,
                                           11 TO 20 BY 5, 9, 7;
                                   A(I) = 0;
                                   END;
```

(d)

```
      J = 4                        J = 4;
      DO 300 I = 1,10              DO I = 1 TO 10 WHILE (J > 0);
      IF (J.LE.0) GO TO 400        A(I) = 0;
      A(I) = 0.                    J = J − I;
300   J = J − I                    END;
400   CONTINUE
```

6. Note the errors in the following DO loops.

```
      DO 400 I = −3, −7, −1        DO I = −3 TO −7 BY −1;
      IF (A(I).EQ.0.) GO TO 500    IF A(I) = 0 THEN GO TO S500;
      DO 400 J = 3,7               DO J = 3 TO 7;
      IF (B(J).EQ.0.) GO TO 600    IF B(J) = 0 THEN GO TO S600;
400   CONTINUE                     END; END;
500   J1 = I                       S500: J1 = I;
      DO 700 J = J1,100,10         DO J = J1 TO 100 BY 10;
600   B(J) = 100.                  S600: B(J) = 100;
```

FORTRAN	PL/I
700 IF (A(I).EQ.7.) GO TO 800	S700: IF A(I) = 7 THEN GO TO S800;
800 CONTINUE	END; S800:

7. Assume that IDY, IMO, and IYR contain the day, month, and year of a start date, and that IDUR contains a duration in days. Assuming 30 days per month, use IF statements and assignment statements to compute the end date from the start date and the duration, and store the results back in IDY, IMO, and IYR.

8. Assume that the day, month, and year of a start date are contained in IDY1, IMO1, and IYR1, and the end date in IDY2, IMO2, and IYR2. Write the statements necessary to store the exact duration in days in IDUR, assuming 30 days per month.

9. An array named AMOUNT has 100 elements. Sum the even elements from 2 up to and including element 50, and every third element from 51 to 100, but stop the summation if the total exceeds 1000.

10. An equation is given as $y = (x - 1)/(x^2 + 1)$. Write the statements necessary to evaluate the equation for values of x ranging from -6 to $+10$ by steps of 0.5.

Chapter 4

Numeric Data Types

Both FORTRAN and PL/I have integer (binary fixed-point) and real (floating-point) numbers. PL/I has in addition decimal fixed-point numbers. All numbers may be signed plus ($+$) or minus ($-$), or unsigned, in which case the number is assumed to be positive.

I. DECIMAL FIXED-POINT NUMBERS

PL/I has *decimal fixed-point* numbers; FORTRAN does not. (Decimal fixed-point numbers are called packed decimal in assembler language, and COMP-3 in COBOL.) Decimal fixed-point numbers are stored in the computer as groups of binary digits or bits, with each group representing a decimal digit. Decimal fixed-point numbers may have a decimal point, and the number of digits to the left and right of the decimal point is fixed.

Decimal fixed-point numbers are less efficient for computation than binary numbers, but they are more efficient for input/output because less conversion is required to change them into character form. They combine the exact precision of binary fixed-point numbers with some of the flexibility of floating-point numbers in allowing a decimal point. They also permit a fairly wide range of values—up to 15 decimal digits on S/360/370.

PL/I

Literals are written as decimal numbers with an optional decimal point.

23   175.925 $-.00973$

Variables must be declared explicitly to be decimal fixed-point by the DCL statement.

DCL (A,B) FIXED(5,4);

The (5,4) specifies 5 total digits with 4 digits to the right of the decimal point (x.xxxx). The general form is (w,d), where w specifies the total number of digits (15 or less on S/360/370), and d the number of digits to the right of the decimal point. If d is omitted, (w,0) is assumed. If (w,d) is omitted, (5,0) becomes the default. DCL can be written in its long form as DECLARE, and FIXED can also be written as FIXED DECIMAL or FIXED DEC. The following two statements are equivalent.

> DCL A FIXED(3), B FIXED;
> DECLARE A FIXED
> > DECIMAL(3,0),
> > B FIXED
> > DECIMAL(5,0);

II. INTEGER (BINARY FIXED-POINT) NUMBERS

Both FORTRAN and PL/I have *binary fixed-point* numbers, termed *integer* numbers in FORTRAN. Binary numbers are stored internally in a computer word as a group of binary digits or bits representing the entire number. Binary numbers are the most efficient numbers for arithmetic computations because computers are binary machines.

Integers can be signed, but they cannot have a decimal point. (For example, 0, −12, 33, but not −1.2 or 3.3.)

Binary fixed-point numbers can be signed, and they can have a decimal point with a fixed number of digits to the left and right of the decimal point.

Literals are written as decimal numbers, without a decimal point.

Binary fixed-point literals are almost impossible to use because they must be written in binary. For example, 2 is written as 10B, and −18 is written as −10010B. Rather than writing binary fixed-point literals, use decimal fixed-point literals and let the computer convert them to binary as needed.

2   −9   18   0

2   −9   18   0   7.42   .006

Variables with names beginning I to N default to full-word integer.

Variables with names beginning I to N default to binary fixed-point with precision (15,0) as described below.

I NONE LIST KEY J

I NONE LIST KEY J

Variables can also be declared explicitly to be integer by the INTEGER statement.

Variables can also be declared explicitly to be binary fixed-point by the DCL statement.

INTEGER A,B,C

DCL (A,B,C) FIXED BIN(31,0);

The (31,0) specifies 31 total bits with 0 bits to the right of the decimal point. The general form is (*w,d*) where *w* is the total number of bits (1 to 31 on S/360/370), and *d* is the number of bits to the right of the decimal point. *d* is assumed to be zero if omitted. (*w,d*) defaults to (15,0) if omitted. FIXED BIN can also be written as FIXED BINARY. The following two statements are equivalent.

> DCL I FIXED BIN(8), J FIXED BIN;
> DECLARE I FIXED BINARY(8,0),
> > J FIXED BINARY(15,0);

FORTRAN	PL/I
Integers are normally stored in full words and most computers allow a maximum magnitude of at least 2,147,483,647. The INTEGER statement can also define half-words (two bytes) with some compilers, for a maximum magnitude of at least 32,767 on most computers.	Values of *w* from 16 to 31 are stored in full words on S/360/370 for a maximum magnitude of 2,147,483,647. Values of *w* from 1 to 15 are stored in half-words on S/360/370 for a maximum magnitude of 32,767.

INTEGER*2 I, J, K   DCL (I, J, K) FIXED BIN(15);

III. REAL (FLOATING-POINT) NUMBERS

Both FORTRAN and PL/I have *floating-point* numbers, called *real* numbers in FORTRAN. Floating-point numbers are stored in a computer word in two parts; one part represents the significant digits of the number, and the other part represents the exponent that determines the magnitude of the number. This corresponds to scientific notation where, for example, .0000025 is represented as .25E−5, and −25000 is represented as −.25E5. This notation allows a wide range of numbers to be used in arithmetic computations without losing significant digits of precision.

Floating-point numbers are not absolutely precise; their precision is limited to some number of significant digits. For example, the result of a computation such as .1 + .1 may yield 0.199999 when expressed in binary, rather than exactly 0.2. This is acceptable in scientific computations where answers are given plus or minus some tolerance, but it can be inappropriate for business applications where numbers may have to balance to the penny.

FORTRAN	PL/I
Literals are written as decimal numbers with a decimal point.	Literals are written as decimal numbers with an optional decimal point, followed by an E, followed by an exponent. Both the number and the exponent may be signed.

2.   −9.   18.3   0.22   2E0   −9E0   18.3E0   2.2E−1

FORTRAN	PL/I
Literals may also be written as decimal numbers with an optional decimal point, followed by an E, followed by an exponent. Both the number and the exponent may be signed.	

7E0 −.97E−16 −22.8E12 −4E−20   7E0 −.97E−16 −22.8E12 −4E−20

FORTRAN	PL/I
Variables with names beginning A to H and O to Z default to single-precision floating-point.	Variables with names beginning A to H, O to Z, $, #, and @ default to floating-point with precision (6) as described below.

A HUGE OUT ZENO   A HUGE OUT ZENO

FORTRAN	PL/I
Variables can be declared explicitly to be floating-point by the REAL Type statement.	Variables can be declared explicitly to be floating-point

REAL I, J, K   DCL (I, J, K) FLOAT(6);

The (6) specifies six decimal digits of precision. The general form is (d), and d can range from 1 to 16 on S/360/370; 1 to 6 is single precision and 7 to 16 is double precision. d defaults to 6 if not specified. FLOAT can also be written as FLOAT DECIMAL or FLOAT DEC. The following two statements are equivalent.

> DCL A FLOAT;
> DECLARE A FLOAT DECIMAL(6);

Floating-point numbers occupy a full word. (Double-precision numbers are described in the next section.) Most computers allow a maximum magnitude of at least 10^{-38} to 10^{38}, and at least six decimal digits of precision.

Values of d from 1 to 6 occupy full words on S/360/370, and have a maximum magnitude of 10^{-78} to 10^{75}. (The following section describes double-precision numbers.)

IV. DOUBLE-PRECISION FLOATING-POINT NUMBERS

Double-precision floating-point numbers have roughly twice the precision of normal floating-point numbers, and are stored in a double word in the computer.

Literals are written as decimal numbers, with an optional decimal point, followed by a D, followed by the exponent. Both the number and the exponent may be signed.

Literals are written the same as normal floating-point numbers, with a decimal number, an optional decimal point, followed by an E, followed by an exponent. Both the number and the exponent may be signed.

> 2D0 $-.97$D-16 -22.8D12

> 2E0 $-.97$E-16 -22.8E12

Variables are specified to be double precision by the DOUBLE PRECISION or the REAL*8 statement. The following two statements are equivalent.

Variables are specified to be double precision by giving the variable a precision of (16) in the DCL statement.

> DOUBLE PRECISION A,B,C
>
> REAL*8 A,B,C

> DCL (A,B,C) FLOAT DEC(16);

Most computers allow a maximum magnitude of at least 10^{-78} to 10^{75}, and at least 16 decimal digits of precision.

The maximum magnitude on S/360/370 is 10^{-78} to 10^{75}, and 16 decimal digits of precision can be obtained.

V. COMPLEX NUMBERS

Complex numbers consist of a real and an imaginary part.

Literals are written as a pair of floating-point numbers separated by a comma and enclosed in parentheses. The first number is the

Literals are written as a pair of numbers of any numeric data type. The first number is the real part, and is followed by the sign of

FORTRAN	PL/I
real part, and the second is the imaginary part.	the imaginary part, the imaginary part, and the letter I.
$(3.2, -1.86)$ $(-5.1E3, .16E2)$	$3.2 - 1.86I$ $-5.1E3 - .16E2I$
Variables are specified to be complex by the COMPLEX Type statement.	Variables are specified to be complex by adding the key word COMPLEX to the DCL statement for any numeric data type.
COMPLEX A,B,C	DCL (A,B,C) COMPLEX FLOAT;
Complex numbers default to single precision real (*8). They can also be defined as double precision (*16).	Complex numbers can be of any data type, and the precision is specified in the DCL statement. Double-precision floating-point numbers are declared as follows.
COMPLEX*16 A,B,C	DCL (A,B,C) COMPLEX FLOAT(16);
Complex numbers cannot appear in any logical expression, such as the logical IF statement.	Complex numbers can only appear in comparisons for equal (=) and not equal (¬=) in logical expressions such as the IF statement.

A. Real Function

FORTRAN	PL/I
The real part of a complex number is obtained by the REAL function (or DREAL for double-precision numbers), or by the assignment statement.	The real part of a complex number is obtained by the REAL function, or by the assignment statement. The result is the same data type as the argument.
REAL((7.0,5.0)) yields 7.0 DREAL((7D0,5D0)) yields 7D0 A = (7.0,5.0) yields 7.0	REAL(7E0 + 5E0I) yields 7E0 A = 7E0 + 5E0I; yields 7E0

B. IMAG Function

FORTRAN	PL/I
The imaginary part of a complex number is obtained by the AIMAG function (or DIMAG for double-precision numbers).	The imaginary part of a complex number is obtained by the IMAG function. The result is of the same data type as the argument.
AIMAG((7.5,5.)) yields 5. DIMAG((7D0,5D0)) yields 5D0	IMAG(7 + 5I) yields 5

C. Conversion from Real to Complex

FORTRAN	PL/I
A single number is converted to complex with a zero imaginary part by the assignment statement.	A single number is converted to complex with a zero imaginary part by the assignment statement.
C = 7. yields (7.,0.) if C is complex	C = 7; yields 7 + 0I if C is complex

D. CMPLX/COMPLEX Function

Two numbers are converted to complex by the CMPLX function (or DCMPLX for double-precision numbers).

Two numbers are converted to complex by the COMPLEX function. The result is of the same data type as the argument.

    CMPLX(7.,5.) yields (7.,5.)
    DCMPLX(7D0,5D0)
                    yields (7D0,5D0)

    COMPLEX(7,5) yields $7 + 5I$

E. CONJG Function

The CONJG function (or DCONJG for double-precision numbers) obtains the conjugate of a complex number by reversing the sign of the imaginary part.

The CONJG function obtains the conjugate of a complex number by reversing the sign of the imaginary part.

    CONJG((7.,5.)) yields (7.,-5.)
    DCONJG((7D0,5D0))
                  yields (7D0,-5D0)

    CONJG($7 + 5I$) yields $7 - 5I$

VI. EXERCISES

1. Which numeric data types are the following literals?

2	2
22E7	22E7
7.6	7.6
(7.,2.)	$7 + 2I$
$-9725.$	$-9725.$
2D4	2E4

2. What will be the results of the following statements?

COMPLEX A,D,E	DCL (A,D,E) COMPLEX FLOAT;
A = (1.,2.)	A = 1E0 + 2E0I;
B = A	B = A;
C = AIMAG(A)	C = IMAG(A);
D = CONJG(CMPLX(2.,	D = CONJG(COMPLEX(2E0,
-3.))	-3E0));
E = 22749.	E = 22749E0;

3. The equation for force as a function of mass and acceleration is given by $f = ma$. Write the statements necessary to define variables named FORCE, MASS, and ACCEL to enable the equation to be solved with decimal fixed-point (PL/I only), binary fixed-point, floating-point, and double-precision floating-point numbers.

4. Select the data types that would be best for the following applications, and describe the reasons why they would be best.

(a) An accounting system.
(b) A table containing the population of states.
(c) Computing rocket trajectories.
(d) Computing the interest on a house loan.
(e) Calculating a table of cube roots.

Chapter 5

Nonnumeric Data Types

I. LOGICAL (BIT-STRING) DATA

FORTRAN *logical* data is used to store the results of decisions that can be answered true or false, or yes or no. PL/I *bit-string* data serves the same purpose, and also provides some of the capability for manipulating individual bits in core storage generally associated with assembler language.

FORTRAN   PL/I

A. Logical (Bit-String) Variables

Logical variables must be declared with the LOGICAL Type statement.

There are no logical variables in PL/I, but a bit-string of length 1 serves the same purpose. A bit-string is a group of binary digits (0 or 1) enclosed in single quotes and followed by a B ('01101'B). Bit-strings must be declared by the DCL statement. In the following example, the BIT(1) specifies a bit-string of length 1. Bit-strings can have any length up to 32,767 on S/360/370.

LOGICAL A,B,C

DCL (A,B,C) BIT(1);

FORTRAN logical variables normally occupy a full word. They can be made to occupy one byte by appending *1 to the LOGICAL statement.

Bit-string storage is allocated in bytes, with up to eight bits per byte on S/360/370.

LOGICAL*1 A,B,C

Logical variables can have values of .TRUE. or .FALSE.

Bit-strings can have values of '1'B (true) or '0'B (false).

A = .TRUE.
B = .FALSE.

A = '1'B;
B = '0'B;

Logical variables can be assigned initial values. In the following statement, D is assigned the value .TRUE., and E the value .FALSE.

Bit-strings can be assigned initial values. In the following statement, D is assigned the value '1'B, and E the value of '0'B.

LOGICAL D/.TRUE./,
          E/.FALSE./

DCL D BIT(1) INIT('1'B),
     E BIT(1) INIT('0'B);

47

B. Logical Expressions

Logical expressions yield a value of .TRUE. or .FALSE.

$$C = A.AND.B$$
$$A = (X.EQ.Z).OR.(B.GT.A)$$

Logical variables can be tested with the Logical IF statement, and the statement part is executed if the logical variable has a value of .TRUE. The following IF statement transfers to 100 if X contains .TRUE.

$$IF (X) GO TO 100$$

Logical expressions yield a value of '1'B or '0'B.

$$C = A \& B;$$
$$A = (X = Z) \,|\, (B > A);$$

Bit-strings can be tested by the IF statement, and the THEN portion is executed if any bit in the bit-string has a value of '1'B. The following IF statement transfers to S100 if any bit in X contains '1'B.

$$IF\ X\ THEN\ GO\ TO\ S100;$$

Bit-strings, or logical expressions that yield a bit-string of length 1, can be used in arithmetic expressions. A bit-string is treated as a binary fixed-point number in an arithmetic expression; for example, '101'B is a binary fixed-point 5. See Chapter 6 for a full described of conversion. In the following statement, D will equal Y if X equals Z; otherwise D will equal zero.

$$D = (X = Z)*Y;$$

The logical *not* operation (⌐) reverses the bits in a bit-string.

$$D = \neg'101'B; \text{yields '010'B}$$

The logical *and* operation (&) sets bits to 1 if both corresponding bits are 1.

$$D = '101'B \& '001'B; \text{yields '001'B}$$

The logical *or* operation (|) sets corresponding bits to 1 if either bit is 1.

$$D = '101'B \,|\, '001'B; \text{yields '101'B}$$

If two operands are of unequal length, the shorter is extended with zeros. For example, '1101'B & '1'B is the same as '1101'B & '1000'B.

The *concatenation* operation (‖) appends the second bit-string to the end of the first.

$$D = '101'B \parallel '010'B; \text{yields '101010'B}$$

The UNSPEC function returns a varying-length bit-string containing the binary representation of its argument. The following statements result in X containing the 32 bits that make up the characters 'THAT', assuming eight bits per character as on S/360/370.

> DCL X BIT(32);
> X = UNSPEC('THAT');

UNSPEC can also appear as a *pseudo-variable* on the left side of an assignment statement. It then converts the right-hand side to a bit-string, if it is not already, and stores it in the item without conversion. In the following example, the characters 'TEXT' are stored in the variable J without conversion, regardless of the data type of J.

> UNSPEC(J) = 'TEXT';

The LENGTH, INDEX, SUBSTR, and VERIFY functions described in the following section on character data can also be used for bit-strings.

C. Varying-Length Bit-Strings

Not in FORTRAN.

Varying-length bit-strings assume the length of the bit-string assigned to them. They are specified by the VARYING attribute (usually written in its short form, VAR) in the DCL statement. The string length specified is the maximum size of the bit-string. The following statement allows B to contain zero to 10 bits.

> DCL B BIT(10) VAR;

The statement B = '1011'B; would give B a length of 4. The statement B = ''; assigns a null string of length of zero to B.

II. CHARACTER DATA

Character data, termed *character-string* in PL/I and *hollerith* data in FORTRAN, consists of groups of characters. FORTRAN is essentially designed to use character data only for input/output, particularly for printing lines of output. FORTRAN has no character data type; numeric data types must be used to store character data. FORTRAN character literals can appear only in FORMAT, CALL, DATA, and Type statements. As a result, character data is hard to manipulate in FORTRAN. PL/I has a character data type, and character variables and literals can generally appear in the same PL/I statements as other data types. Character data can be compared, subdivided, expanded, combined, and edited.

A. Character Literals

Literals are written by preceding the characters with *n*H, where *n* is the number of characters.

$$2\text{HAT} \quad 4\text{HIT'S} \quad 5\text{HME TO}$$

Several FORTRAN compilers also allow characters to be enclosed in single quotes; a quote character is denoted by two consecutive quotes.

'AT'   'IT''S'   'ME TO'

Literals can appear only in CALL, DATA, and FORMAT statements. Hence one cannot write A = 4HABCD. Instead, one must trick FORTRAN by writing subroutines such as the following to store character literals into variables.

```
SUBROUTINE STORE(J,K)
J = K
RETURN
END
```

The statement CALL STORE(J,4HABCD) would return with J containing 'ABCD'. This indirect method of handling character data typifies the problems of operating on character data in FORTRAN. Some FORTRAN compilers have added special functions to permit character-strings to be handled more directly. In the absence of these, one is usually forced to either trick FORTRAN, as in the unsavory manner shown above, or write assembler language subroutines to manipulate the character data.

Literals are written by enclosing the characters in single quotes; a quote character is denoted by two consecutive quotes.

'AT'   'IT''S'   'ME TO'

Character literals can appear in any PL/I statement.

J = 'ABCD';

B. Character Variables

FORTRAN has no character data type, and other variables must be used, preferably integer. One must know the number of characters per word, (4, 6, 8, or 10, depending on the computer), to allow room for storing the characters. If all the characters cannot be contained in a single word, they must be stored in an array, with 4, 6, 8, or 10 characters stored in each array element, depending

Fixed-length character-string variables are specified by the DCL statement. The *length* of the string is the number of characters which the string is to contain, and may be a maximum of 32,767 in S/360/370. Character data types are defined as CHARACTER in the DCL statement. CHARACTER is usually written in its short form, CHAR. The *length* is the number of characters the string

FORTRAN	PL/I
on the computer.	is to contain.

DIMENSION *variable*

(size),...

or

INTEGER *variable(size)*,...

In the following example, I can contain 12 characters and J can contain 8 characters if the computer word holds 4 characters.

DIMENSION I(3),J(2)

Variables can be given initial values with the DATA statement. The following example for a computer that has four characters per word initializes J1 with the characters 'ABCD'.

DATA J1/4HABCD/

FORTRAN can assign only a single variable at a time to another variable. In the following example, the three elements or array K are each set to 'XXXX'.

INTEGER K(3),

L(3)/3*4HXXXX/

DO 100 J = 1, 3

100   K(J) = L(J)

Arrays that contain character data can be defined. In the following example, AGE is defined as a 6 by 2 array with six elements containing seven characters each. Two words are required to hold the seven characters, assuming a computer with four characters per word.

DIMENSION AGE(6,2)

The third element of the array is assigned the characters 'FIFTEEN':

DATA I/4HFIFT/,J/3HEEN/

AGE(3,1) = I

AGE(3,2) = J

---

is to contain.

DCL *variable* CHAR(*length*);

In the following example, I can contain 12 characters, and J can contain 8 characters.

DCL I CHAR(12), J CHAR(8);

Character-string variables can be given initial values by adding INIT('*string*') to the DCL statement. The following example initializes J1 with the character string 'ABCD'.

DCL J1 CHAR(4) INIT('ABCD');

PL/I can assign character-string variables and literals to another character-string variable. In the following example, K is set to 'XXXXXXXXXXXX'.

DCL K CHAR(12),

L CHAR(12) INIT((12) 'X');

K = L;

In the assignment statement, variables are padded on the right with blanks if they are assigned a smaller character-string; longer strings are truncated on the right.

DCL A CHAR(4);

A = 'AB'; (A contains 'ABbb')

A = 'ABCDEF'; (A contains 'ABCD')

Arrays of character-strings can be defined. In the following example, AGE has six elements, and each element contains seven characters.

DCL AGE(6) CHAR(7);

The third element of the array is assigned the characters 'FIFTEEN':

AGE(3) = 'FIFTEEN';

The initialization of character data is somewhat complex, and the following rules apply.

If too few characters are specified, the word is padded out on the right with blanks. If too many characters are specified, the left characters are truncated. In the following example, J2 contains '1bbb' and J3 contains 'WXYZ'.	If too few characters are specified, the string is padded out on the right with blanks. If too many characters are specified, the right characters are truncated. In the following example, J2 contains '1bbb' and J3 contains 'VWXY'.

FORTRAN:

DATA J2/1H1/,
      J3/5HVWXYZ/

PL/I:

DCL J2 CHAR(4) INIT('1'),
      J3 CHAR(4) INIT('VWXYZ');

In assigning initial values to an array, each successive element is assigned the next item in the data list. An iteration factor of the form *n** placed in front of a literal repeats it *n* times. For example, 2*1HA is equivalent to 1HA,1HA. In the following example, K(1), K(2), and K(3) each contain '1111'.	In assigning initial values to an array, each successive element is assigned the next item in the data list. An iteration factor of the form (*n*) placed in front of a literal string repeats the characters within the string *n* times. For example, ((2)'A') is equivalent to ('AA'). A second iteration factor in front of the first iteration factor repeats the entire string. For example, ((2)(1)'A') is equivalent to ('A','A'). In the following example, K(1), K(2), and K(3) each contain '1111'.

DATA K(3)/3*4H1111/

DCL K(3) CHAR(4) INIT((3)(4)'1');

If the character-string is longer than the word size of the computer, the first element of the array is filled with the leftmost characters, and the remaining characters are ignored. In the following example, K(1) contains 'ABCD', and K(2) and K(3) are not initialized.	If the character-string is longer than the length of the character-string, the characters are truncated on the right. In the following example, K(1) contains 'ABCD', and K(2) and K(3) are not initialized.

DATA
K(3)/12HABCDEFGHIJKL/

DCL K(3) CHAR(4)
      INIT('ABCDEFGHIJKL');

The WATFIV FORTRAN compiler permits character variables to be defined by the CHARACTER data type. The *name* is the name of the variable, and *length* is the number of characters (maximum of 255) that the variable is to contain.

CHARACTER *name*length*,
      *name*length*,...
or
CHARACTER**length*
      name,name,...

The CHARACTER data type may also appear in IMPLICIT and FUNCTION statements. WATFIV also permits literal character-strings to appear in assignment and IF statements. (Like PL/I, WATFIV pads the shorter string on the right with blanks if necessary to make the two strings of equal length for the comparison.)

CHARACTER A*8	DCL A CHAR(8);
A = 'START IT'	A = 'START IT';
IF (A.EQ.'NOT DONE')	IF A = 'NOT DONE' THEN
GO TO 1000	GO TO S1000;

C. Character-String Expressions

FORTRAN will try to perform arithmetic conversion if variables of a different type appear in the same statement. In the following statement, FORTRAN assumes that J is an integer and tries to convert it to floating-point to assign it to the floating-point variable A. The results are meaningless if J contains characters.

A = J (Wrong!)

The IF statement can compare two variables containing character data. The IF statement compares the variables as if they were integer or real variables. A variable containing four characters per word can compare only four characters at a time with the IF statement. Be careful not to compare mixed modes or FORTRAN will perform arithmetic conversion on the character data, yielding meaningless results. In the following example, the characters 'ABCD' are compared to '23bb'.

The IF statement can compare two character-strings. The two strings are compared character by character from left to right according to the collating sequence of the computer. If the strings are of unequal length, the shorter is padded on the right with blanks to equal the length of the longer string for the comparison. In the following example, the characters 'ABCD' are compared to '23bb'.

DATA J1/4HABCD/,	DCL J1 CHAR(4) INIT('ABCD'),
J2/4H23bb/	J2 CHAR(2) INIT('23'));
IF (J1.EQ.J2) GO TO 100	IF J1 = J2 THEN GO TO S100;

The IF statement treats the word containing characters as an integer or real variable for the comparison, and the comparison may not give the results one would expect from the collating sequence of the characters. For example, on some computers the character 'A' occupies eight bits and is represented as

1100 0001 and the character 'Z' is represented as 1110 1001. If either character is the leftmost character in a word, the leftmost bit is a 1, which indicates to the computer that the number is negative. Thus in the following example, I2 is less than I1 even though Z is larger than A, because I1 and I2 appear to the computer as negative integers.

DATA I1/4HAbbb/,
        I2/4HZbbb/
IF (I2.LT.I1) GO TO 100

Character-strings can be concatenated to append one character-string to the end of another.

'AB' ‖ 'BC' yields 'ABBC'
B = 'WALLA';
B = B ‖ 'b' ‖ B; yields
                'WALLAbWALLA'

D.   Varying-Length Character-Strings

Not in FORTRAN.

Varying-length character-strings assume the length of the character-string assigned to them. They are specified by the VARYING attribute (usually written in its short form VAR) in the DCL statement. The string length is the maximum size of the character-string. In the following example, B can contain from 0 to 100 characters.

DCL B CHAR(100) VAR;

The statement B = 'THIS'; would give B a length of 4. The statement B = ''; assigns a null string to B of zero length.

The function LENGTH(*string*) returns the current *length* of the varying-length *string*.

B = 'AB'; I = LENGTH(B);
                (I equals 2)
B = ''; I = LENGTH(B);
                (I equals 0)

The function INDEX(*string*, '*characters*') searches a *string* for the first instance of a specified group of *characters* and returns the number of the first character of the match, or zero if there is no match.

```
B = 'IS IT, OR IS IT NOT?';
I = INDEX(B,'IT'); (I equals 4)
I = INDEX(B,'Z'); (I equals 0)
```

The function SUBSTR(*string,n^{th},number*) copies the given *number* of characters from the *string*, starting with the nth character.

```
C = 'IT IS I';
D = SUBSTR(C,4,2);
                (D contains 'IS')
```

The length can be omitted, and characters are copied from the starting character to the end of the string.

```
D = SUBSTR(C,2);
                (D contains 'T IS I')
```

The SUBSTR function can examine specific characters in a string. The sixth character of string C is examined to determine if it is an 'A' in the following example.

```
IF SUBSTR(C,6,1) = 'A' THEN GO
                TO START;
```

The SUBSTR function can appear as a *pseudovariable* on the left-hand side of the assignment statement. It stores a given *number* of characters from the string on the right side into the nth and following positions of the *string* named in the SUBSTR function on the left side.

```
C = 'MARY IS';
SUBSTR(C,1,4) = 'JOAN';
                (C contains 'JOAN IS')
```

SUBSTR is relatively inefficient. As an alternative, substrings can be defined with the DEF and POS options described in Chapter 7, often obviating the need for SUBSTR.

```
DCL A CHAR(80);
DCL X CHAR(6);
X = SUBSTR(A,60,6);
    or
DCL A CHAR(80),
    B CHAR(6) DEF A POS(60);
DCL X CHAR(6);
X = B;
```

The VERIFY(*string,pattern-string*) function determines if each character in the first *string* appears somewhere in the *pattern-string*. A value of zero is returned if all characters are found; otherwise the position of the first character in the *string* not to match is returned. The VERIFY function can examine a character-string to determine if it contains only specified characters. The following example checks a string to determine if it contains only numeric digits.

DCL A CHAR(6);
A = '253769';
I = VERIFY(A,'0123456789');

(I equals 0)

A = '257A69';
I = VERIFY(A,'0123456789');

(I equals 4)

III. EXERCISES

1. Define two logical variables named YES and NO, and initialize YES to a value of true and NO to a value of false.

2. What will the following data items contain if initialized by the following statements?

INTEGER CH(2),L,   DCL CH(3) CHAR(4)
  M(3)/6H123456,2*2HZZ,   INIT((2)(3)'X','123456');
    1H9,2*5H54321/

3. An array named NAME has 100 elements, and each element contains four characters. Count the occurrences of the characters 'ABCD' and 'DCBA' in the array.

4. Define three logical variables, HOLIDY, RAIN, and WINDY. Then define an integer variable MONEY and a floating-point variable TEMP. Assume that all variables have been set to some initial value such that if HOLIDY is true it is a holiday, if RAIN is true it is raining, if WINDY is true it is windy, and MONEY is an amount of money and TEMP is the temperature. Define a logical variable DAY and set it to true or false based on the following sentence. If it is a holiday and it is not raining and windy and if we have over $100 in money, and if the temperature is greater than 70 but less than 85, then it is a good day. Otherwise it is a bad day. Let the value of DAY be true if it is a good day.

5. The following IF statement has been coded.

IF (IS.NE.0.AND.IA.EQ.1   IF IS ¬= 0 & IA = 1 & IS ¬= 1 |
  .AND.IS.NE.1.OR.IS.NE.2)   IS ¬= 2 THEN GO TO S100;
    GO TO 100

Tell whether the transfer will be made to statement 100 based on the following combinations of values of IS and IA.

IA	IS
0	0
0	1
0	2
0	3
1	0
1	1
1	2
1	3

6. (PL/I only). Define a bit-string of length 1 named FLAG and set it to true if the first eight bits of a character-string named REC are all 1's.

7. (PL/I only). What will A and B contain as a result of the following statements?

```
DCL A CHAR(6) VAR, B BIT(6);
A = SUBSTR('THAT',2,2);
A = A || 'Z' || SUBSTR('XX''XXXX',
                                    1,4);
B = ¬('110111'B & '00101'B);
```

Chapter 6

Data Conversion

I. AUTOMATIC DATA CONVERSION

Data conversion occurs automatically when operations are performed on different data types. The data is converted to a common base to perform the operations. The assignment statement also results in conversion if the variable on the left differs from the data type of the results on the right. Arithmetic precision can be lost during conversion in the low-order digits. Precision in an assignment statement can also be lost in both the high- and low-order digits if the variable on the left cannot contain the number on the right. The loss of high-order digits can be detected as described in Chapter 11, but the loss in low-order digits is not detected. Conversion also takes computer time, and excessive conversion can make a program run slow.

A. Hierarchy of Conversion

The following list shows the hierarchy of conversion, from lowest to highest. For example, if a bit-string, a binary fixed-point number, and a double-precision number appear in the same expression, the bit-string and the binary fixed-point number are converted to double precision to perform the operation.

FORTRAN	PL/I
Lowest to highest:	Lowest to highest:
—	Bit-string
—	Character-string
Integer	Binary fixed-point
—	Decimal fixed-point
Real	Floating-point
Double-precision real	Double-precision floating-point
Complex	Complex

B. Conversion to Integer

Floating-point numbers (and PL/I decimal fixed-point numbers) are truncated to integer, not rounded. For example, 1.9 is truncated to 1.

C. Conversion to Floating-Point

Integers (and PL/I decimal fixed-point numbers) are converted to floating-point, rounding to the number of significant digits provided on the computer. For example, A = 146769826 yields roughly 1.46770E8 on a computer with six floating-point digits of precision.

Double-precision floating-point numbers are truncated to single-precision floating-point numbers. For example, the number 1.46769826E8 is truncated to 1.46769E8 on a computer with six decimal digits of floating-point precision.

D.   Conversion to Double-Precision Floating-Point

Numbers are converted to single-precision floating-point if they are not already in this form, and are then extended on the right with zeros to fill the double-precision word. For example, the number 1.46769E8 is expanded to roughly 1.46769000000E8 on a computer with six floating-point digits of precision.

E.   Conversion to Complex

The number is converted to the data type of the complex number, and the result is assigned to the real part of the complex number. The imaginary part of the complex number is set to zero.

$$C = 5. \text{ (yields } (5.,0.)) \qquad\qquad C = 5; \text{ (yields } 5+0I)$$

F.   Conversion from Complex

The imaginary part of the complex number is ignored, and the real part is converted as a normal number.

$$A = (5.,7.) \text{ (yields } 5.) \qquad\qquad A = 5.+7.I; \text{ (yields } 5)$$

G.   Conversion from Bit-String to Character-String

Bit-strings are not in FORTRAN.

Each bit is converted to the character '0' or '1'; for example, '101'B becomes '101'. In an assignment statement, the resulting character-string is truncated on the right if too long, or padded on the right with blanks if too short.

DCL A BIT(4) INIT('1011'B),
                    B CHAR(3);
B = A; (yields '1011', which is truncated to '101'.)

H.   Conversion from Character-String to Bit-String

Bit-strings are not in FORTRAN.

Each '0' or '1' character is converted of a 0 or 1 bit. (Character-strings converted to bit-strings can contain only '0' or '1's.) For example, '101' becomes '101'B. In an assignment statement, the resulting bit-string is truncated on the right if too long, or extended on the right with zeros if too short.

DCL A CHAR(4) INIT('1011'),
                    B BIT(5);
B = A; (yields '1011'B, which is extended to '10110'B.)

I. Conversion from Bit-String to Arithmetic

Bit-strings are not in FORTRAN.

The bit-string is converted to a binary fixed-point number, and is then converted from binary fixed-point to the required data type.

> DCL A FIXED DECIMAL;
> A = '101'B; (yields the binary fixed-
> point number 5, which is
> in turn converted to a
> decimal 5.)

J. Conversion from Arithmetic to Bit-String

Bit-strings are not in FORTRAN.

The integer part of the number is converted to binary fixed-point, and the binary fixed-point number is then converted to a bit-string. The length of the bit-string varies with the data type. The lengths shown below are for S/360/370.

TYPE	Length of Bit-String
FIXED(w,d)	(w−d)*3.32, rounded up to integer.
FLOAT(w)	w*3.32, rounded up to integer.
FIXED BIN(w,d)	w−d

> DCL A FIXED(3,1) INIT(7.9),
> B BIT(5);
> B = A; (yields '0000111', which is trun-
> cated to '00001'.)

K. Conversion from Character to Arithmetic

Not in FORTRAN.

The character-string is treated as though it were a literal. Blanks can surround the number, but they cannot separate the sign from the value. (A character-string containing only blanks will result in a conversion error. It must contain at least one numeric character.) If the character-string must be converted to an intermediate data type, as would occur if a binary fixed-point literal were assigned to a floating-point variable, it is first converted to decimal fixed-point with precision (15,0) and any fractional part will be lost.

L.   Conversion from Arithmetic to Character

Not in FORTRAN.

Binary fixed-point numbers of precision (w,d) are first converted to decimal numbers with precision of $(1+w/3.32,d/3.32)$ on S/360/370. Each item is rounded up to the nearest integer, and conversion then proceeds as for decimal numbers. Decimal numbers of precision (w,d) are converted to character-strings of length $(w+3)$, right justified. For example, DCL A FIXED(6,2) INIT (-706.24); is converted to 'bb-706.24'. The following example converts a binary fixed-point number to character and stores the results in B.

> DCL A FIXED BIN(15)
>
> INIT(-5032),
>
> B CHAR(6);
>
> B = A; (A is first converted to -5032 as a decimal number with precision (5,0), and is then converted to 'bbb-5032', which is in turn truncated to 'bbb-50'.)

Floating-point numbers of precision (w) are converted to a character-string of length $(w+6)$. For example, DCL A FLOAT(6) INIT($-.00021$E0); is converted to 'bbbb-2.1E-04'.

Complex numbers are converted as two numbers according to the data type of the number. The length of the resulting character-string is the sum of the two resulting character-strings, plus 1.

> DCL A COMPLEX FIXED(4,3)
>
> INIT($.947+.221$I),
>
> B CHAR(17);
>
> B = A; (yields 'bbb0.947$+0.221$I', which is padded to 'bbb0.947$+0.221$Ibb'.)

II.   INTERNAL INPUT/OUTPUT CONVERSION

Internal I/O conversion permits character-strings to be converted to numeric, or arithmetic variables to be converted to character-strings, in the same way that I/O records are converted under format control as they are read or written. The internal I/O conversion causes a character-string to be read or written from core rather than from an I/O device.

The READ/WRITE 99 statement is provided by a few compilers to convert data under format control. There is no standard, but usually a separate subroutine call is required to set up the array that contains the characters for a READ statement, or is to contain the characters for a WRITE statement. A READ or WRITE statement with I/O unit 99 is then written the same as for normal I/O as described in Chapter 10. Check with the installation to see if the feature is provided, and if so, how it is used. The WATFIV FORTRAN compiler provides in-core READ and WRITE statements as follows:

> READ (*variable, fmt*) list
> WRITE (*variable, fmt*) list

The following statements illustrate the use of the WATFIV in-core READ and WRITE statements.

```
              CHARACTER
                     A*8/'2.57.668'/,B*9
              READ (A,100) C,D
100           FORMAT(F3.1,F5.3)
        (C contains 2.5 and D contains 7.668)
              WRITE (B,200) D,C
200           FORMAT(F5.3,1X,F3.1)
        (B contains '7.668b2.5')
```

The GET/PUT STRING statements read or write character-strings under format control. The general form is:
> GET STRING(*string*) EDIT
> $\qquad$ (*variable-list*) (*format-list*);
> PUT STRING(*string*) EDIT
> $\qquad$ (*variable-list*) (*format-list*);

GET STRING converts the characters in the *string* according to the *format-list* and stores them in the *variable-list*. PUT STRING converts the *variable-list* to characters according to the *format-list* and stores them in the *string*. The *variable-list* and *format-list* are described in Chapter 10.

The following statements illustrate the use of GET and PUT STRING.

```
        DCL A CHAR(8) INIT('2.57.668'),
              B CHAR(9);
        GET STRING(A) EDIT(C,D)
              (F(3,1),F(5,3));
        (C contains 2.5 and D contains 7.668)
        PUT STRING(B) EDIT(D,C)
              (F(5,3),X(1),F(3,1));
        (B contains '7.668b2.5')
```

III. ACCURACY OF ARITHMETIC COMPUTATIONS

Arithmetic computations are performed by converting the items that appear in an arithmetic expression to a common data base according to the conversion hierarchy given earlier in this chapter. In logical expressions, such as in an IF statement, one of the two expressions will, if necessary, be converted to the base of the other according to the hierarchy. In an assignment statement, the result of an arithmetic operation is converted to the data type of the variable on the left side of the statement. The precision with which the result is stored is the precision of the variable on the left side of the assignment statement. The precision with which numbers are stored is not necessarily the same as the accuracy. The precision of a variable may be double precision, but the accuracy of the number it contains may be single precision. Some of the problems of accuracy are shown in the following examples.

The statement I = (12577944 + 2.5E3)/2 is evaluated as follows, assuming a computer with six decimal digits of floating-point precision.

1. All numbers are converted to floating-point because it has the highest hierarchy of any data type in the expression. The expression becomes in effect: I = (1.25779E7 + 2.5E3)/2E0.

Low-order significant digits were lost when 12577944 was converted to floating-point, assuming a computer with six decimal digits of floating-point precision.

2.   The expression is then evaluated to yield a result of 6.29023E6.

3.   The 6.29023E6 is converted and truncated to integer, and the result of 6290230 is stored in I. (In PL/I, binary fixed-point integers default to precision (15,0) for a maximum magnitude of only 32,767. Had I not been specifically declared to have greater precision, high-order significant digits would be lost for a meaningless result.)

The above is a worst-case example. Different number bases or different values in the computations might yield more accurate results. However, the worst case should always be the accuracy stated for the results of computations.

The truncation of floating-point numbers to integer can yield surprising results. Computers store numbers internally in a numeric base other than the base 10 (decimal) to which we are accustomed. The bases 2 (binary), 8 (octal), and 16 (hexadecimal) are all common. Some numbers that can be expressed exactly in decimal, such as 0.1, might not be expressed exactly in another numeric base, and might be effectively stored as 0.099999, in much the same manner that the fraction $\frac{1}{3}$ is expressed as 0.333333 in decimal. The result can be that a simple statement such as I = 0.1*10.0 might result in a value of zero for I. The computer may be actually dealing with the number 0.099999 rather than 0.1, and 0.099999*10.0 yields 0.999990, which becomes zero when truncated to integer. This type of error is easy to commit, and very hard to detect.

Double-precision constants are another example of the problems that can be encountered in conversion. If A and B are double-precision floating-point numbers, the expression $(A+B)*0.1E0$ may yield a double-precision result with single-precision accuracy. The 0.1E0 may be stored as $0.999999E-1$, and this constant is expanded to double precision by extending it with zeros to become $0.999999000000E-1$, whereas the double-precision constant of 0.1E0 would be $0.999999999999E-1$. Thus one of the items in the expression has only single-precision accuracy, and the expression can be only as accurate as its least accurate component. This mistake is also easy to commit and hard to detect. FORTRAN provides a double-precision constant (.1D0) to solve this problem, but PL/I requires that all significant digits of precision be written out in constants (0.100000000000E0).

Intermediate results in arithmetic computations can also cause problems. For example, a simple statement such as L = I*J/K may yield wrong results. If I contains 100,000, J contains 200,000, and K contains 300,000, the statement yields a meaningless result. This is because the statement is evaluated from left to right as (I*J)/K, and I*J yields 20,000,000,000; a number too large to be contained as an integer. Fixed-point overflow occurs, and the result is meaningless. By changing the equation to I*(J/K), the division occurs before the multiplication, and no overflow occurs. But now the result is zero because J/K yields zero. One must force the computations to be done in floating-point by changing one of the variables to floating-point. Problems caused by intermediate results are particularly vexing. A program may run correctly with test data, and run correctly for years with real data. Then unusual data may suddenly cause fixed-point overflow, or a result of zero as above.

IV. EXERCISES

1.   Give the results of the following expressions.

I = (7.5+4/2.99)/2	I = (7.5E0+4/2.99E0)/2;
A = (7.5+4/2.99)/2	A = (7.5E0+4/2.99E0)/2;

FORTRAN   PL/I

$$J = 4**2+6.7/3$$
$$B = 2/3+7/4-9/4$$

J = 4**2+6.7E0/3;
B = 2/3+7/4−9/4;
DCL C CHAR(6), D BIT(2),
                                    E CHAR(6);

C = 'Z';
D = C = 'Z';

2. Write all the statements, including declaratives, necessary to evaluate the following arithmetic expression with double-precision accuracy.

$$\text{ANS} = \frac{\left(A^{C/4} + \dfrac{B}{3}\right)(Y + 2X)}{\left(B{\cdot}A - \dfrac{W}{Z}\right)^{N-1}}$$

3. The equation for a future amount invested at $i\%$ per year for n years is given by:

$$\text{future amount} = \text{investment}\left(1 + \frac{i}{100}\right)^n$$

Write the statements necessary to compute the future amount of 10-year investments ranging from \$100 to \$102 by increments of 5¢ at an interest rate of $7\frac{1}{4}\%$.

Chapter 7

Data Declaration and Storage

Storage can be allocated for single variables, for arrays, or, in the case of PL/I, for structures. Storage is not automatically set to zero or blanks, but must be initialized or assigned a value before it can be used in computations.

I. DATA DECLARATIONS

The Type statement in FORTRAN, and the DECLARE statement in PL/I are used to declare all data types except those allowed to default to integer (binary fixed-point) by the name beginning with I to N, or to real (floating-point) by the name beginning with A to H or O to Z. (also $, @, and # in PL/I). Arrays can also be defined, and both variables and arrays can be assigned initial values. (The FORTRAN DOUBLE PRECISION statement can also declare data; it is described in Chapter 4.)

FORTRAN
PL/I

A. Explicit Data Type Specification

The general form of the Type statement is as follows.

$$type*n \; v1,v2,...$$

The general form of the DECLARE statement is as follows.

$$DECLARE \; (v1,v2,...) \; type(precision)$$
$$attributes,$$
$$(w1,w2,...) \; type(precision)$$
$$attributes, ...;$$

The type can be INTEGER, REAL, LOGICAL, or COMPLEX. The *n specifies the size in bytes of the data item. The *n is usually omitted, and COMPLEX defaults to *8; INTEGER, REAL, and LOGICAL default to *4. COMPLEX can also be specified as *16, REAL as *8, INTEGER as *2, and LOGICAL as*1. $v1,v2,...$ represent data names.

DECLARE is usually written in its short form as DCL. The usual *types* are FIXED, FIXED BIN, FLOAT, COMPLEX, BIT, and CHAR. The *attributes* include EXTERNAL, DEFINED, STATIC, CONTROLLED, etc. $v1,v2,w1,w2$ represent data names. Single items need not be enclosed in parentheses.

REAL A,B,C
INTEGER D

DCL (A,B,C) FLOAT,
D FIXED BIN;

The DOUBLE PRECISION statement is equivalent to the REAL*8 statement, and is used to define double-precision floating-point variables.

DOUBLE PRECISION
A,B,C

DCL (A,B,C) FLOAT(16);

B. Implicit/Default Data Type Specification

The Implicit and DEFAULT statements override the normal default for names in which those beginning with I to N default to integer (binary fixed-point) and those beginning with A to H, O to Z (also $, #, and @ in PL/I) default to real (floating-point).

There can be only one IMPLICIT statement per program or subroutine, which must be the first statement within the routine. In the following example, names beginning with A or B are made to default to integer, and names beginning with I default to real.

IMPLICIT INTEGER(A,B),
REAL(I)

ABLE(integer)   BAKER(integer)
COST(real)   IX(real)   J(integer)

The IMPLICIT statement can also specify a range of characters to default. In the following example, names beginning with W, X, Y, and Z default to real.

IMPLICIT REAL(W – Z)

The DEFAULT statement is available on only a few PL/I compilers. There may be several DEFAULT statements within a procedure, and there are no restrictions on their placement. In the following example, names beginning with A or B default to binary fixed-point, and names beginning with I default to floating-point.

DEFAULT RANGE(A,B) FIXED
BINARY,
RANGE(I) FLOAT;

ABLE(binary fixed)
BAKER(binary fixed)
COST(floating-point)
IX(floating-point)   J(binary fixed)

The DEFAULT statement can also specify a range of characters to default. In the following example, names beginning with W, X, Y, and Z default to floating-point.

DEFAULT RANGE(W – Z) FLOAT;

The default can be set for all names that begin with a series of characters. In the following example, all names that begin with STO, such as STOP, STORE, and STOA, would default to decimal fixed-point.

DEFAULT RANGE(STO) FIXED;

The default for all names can be set by coding an asterisk. In the following example, the default for all names is set to floating-point.

DEFAULT RANGE(*) FLOAT;

The IMPLICIT statement can specify the precision by coding one of the following as the data type: INTEGER, INTEGER*2, REAL, REAL*8, LOGICAL, LOGICAL*1,

Unless the precision is specified with a VALUE clause, the precision is the system default; binary fixed-point is precision (15,0), floating-point is precision (6), and

COMPLEX, or COMPLEX*16. In the following example, names beginning with B to E and X default to double precision.

decimal fixed-point is precision (5,0). The VALUE clause sets a specific precision, and it must be used for CHAR and BIT to specify the string length. In the following example, names beginning with B to E and X default to floating-point with precision (16).

IMPLICIT REAL*8(B – E,X)

DEFAULT RANGE(B – E,X)
                FLOAT VALUE(FLOAT(16));

Any subsequent Type statements override the defaults set by the IMPLICIT statement.

Any subsequent DCL statements override the defaults set by the DEFAULT statement.

IMPLICIT REAL*8(E,
                W – Z),LOGICAL(A)

DEFAULT RANGE(E,W – Z)
                FLOAT VALUE(FLOAT(16)),
                RANGE(A) BIT
                            VALUE(BIT(1));

INTEGER WAY
EXTRA(real*8)   WHERE(real*8)
WAY(integer)   AT(logical)

DCL WAY FIXED BIN;
EXTRA(float(16))   WHERE(float(16))
WAY(binary fixed)   AT(bit(1))

The INIT attribute can assign initial values to default names. In the following example, names beginning with M default to CHAR and are initialized to blanks.

DEFAULT RANGE(M) CHAR
                VALUE(CHAR(4)) INIT(‘   ’);

II. ARRAYS

A. Array Specifications

Arrays may have up to three dimensions. (Many compilers allow seven.)

Arrays may have up to 15 dimensions. (S/360/370 permits up to 32.)

A(1,2,3,4,5,6,7)

A(1,2,3,4,5,6,7,...,32)

Arrays are specified by the DIMENSION, COMMON, Type, or DOUBLE PRECISION statements. In the following examples, A is defined as a 2 by 10 array, and I as a 1 by 30 array. The bounds are from 1 to n, where n is the maximum value specified; for example, A(1,1) to A(2,10), and I(1) to I(30).

Arrays are specified by the DCL statement. In the following example, A is defined as a 2 by 10 array, and I as a 1 by 30 array. The bounds are from 1 to n, where n is the maximum value specified; for example, A(1,1) to A(2,10), and I(1) to I(30).

DIMENSION A(2,10),I(30)
COMMON A(2,10),I(30)
REAL A(2,10),I(30)
DOUBLE PRECISION
A(2,10),I(30)

DCL A(2,10) FLOAT, I(30) FIXED
BIN;

The bounds can also be specified by a pair of numbers in the form (*min :max*), and in addition can have negative or zero values. In the following example, array B has 10 values from B(1971) to B(1980), array C has 16 values from C(-10) to C(5), and array D has 6 values from D(0) to D(5).

DCL B(1971 :1980), C(-10:5), D(0:5);

Dimensions of arrays can also be specified with variables or expressions unless the array is defined as STATIC (see following section.) The value of the variable or expression when the DCL statement is encountered determines the bounds of the array. Noninteger variables and expressions are truncated to integer.

I = 7; J = 2.8;
DCL A(I+J); (Same as DCL A(9);)

Arrays are stored in *column-major* order, with the leftmost subscript increasing most rapidly. DIMENSION A(2,2) is stored as:

A(1,1), A(2,1), A(1,2), A(2,2)

Arrays are stored in *row-major* order, with the rightmost subscript increasing most rapidly. DCL A(2,2); is stored as:

A(1,1), A(1,2), A(2,1), A(2,2)

Subscripts must be positive, nonzero integer constants, variables, or expressions. Most compilers allow any integer expressions, but some allow only the following, where c and k are integer constants and v is an integer variable:

$c*v+k$ $c*v-k$ $c*v$
$v+k$ $v-k$ v k
A(1), A(I), A(2,I + 3), A(4*J), but not A(2,3 + I) or A(J*4)

Subscripts can be any numeric constants, variables, or expressions. Noninteger values are truncated to integer.

A(1), A(I), A(2,I + 3), A(I*2 + 3,8 + J),
A(0), A(-3), A(B*C $-$ D/6)
A(22.6) (Same as A(22))

B. Array Expressions

FORTRAN does not have array expressions. If an array appears in an expression without a subscript, FORTRAN assumes that the

PL/I has array expressions that permit operations on an entire array in a single statement. When an array appears in an first element of the array is meant. For example, A is the same as A(1).

expression without a subscript, the operation is performed on the entire array, element-by-element. If two arrays appear in an expression, the operation is performed on the corresponding elements of each array, and the arrays must have identical bounds. In an operation involving an array and a scalar, the scalar operates on each element of the array. The result of an array expression is an array having the same bounds, and the left-hand side of the assignment statement must be an array of identical bounds if an array expression appears on the right-hand side.

```
      DIMENSION A(20),B(20)
      DO 100 I = 1, 20
100   A(I) = B(I) + 2.0
      DO 200 I = 1, 20
200   B(I) = 0.
```

```
DCL (A,B) (20);
A = B + 2E0;

B = 0E0;
```

Cross-sections of arrays are operated upon by using an asterisk (*) as a subscript. This causes an expression to be performed for all values (cross-section) of that dimension.

```
      DIMENSION A(10,20)
      DO 300 I = 1, 20
300   A(2,I) = 0.
```

```
DCL A(10,20);
A(2,*) = 0E0;
```

III.   DATA INITIALIZATION

Initial values are assigned to items in the Type statement by following the name (and any array dimensions) with the value enclosed in slashes. The value assigned should match the data type of the name; no conversion is performed if it does not match.

Initial values are assigned to items in the DCL statement by following the *type* (*precision*) with the INITIAL attribute (usually written in its short form as INIT.) The value assigned should match the data type of the name; conversion is performed if it does not match.

REAL A/2./

DCL A FLOAT(6) INIT(2E0);

A list of names can be initialized by a corresponding list of values.

A list of names cannot be initialized by a corresponding list of values.

REAL A,B,C/2.,3.,4./

```
DCL (A,B,C) INIT(2E0,3E0,4E0);
Wrong! Must be written as follows:
DCL A INIT(2E0), B INIT(3E0),
                    C INIT(4E0);
```

71

An iteration factor $n*$ can be appended to a value, causing it to be repeated n times. /3*0/ is the same as /0,0,0/.

The DATA statement assigns values to arrays specified by the DIMENSION statement, and to variables that assume the default data types based on the first character of their name. Names and values are written for the DATA statement in the same way in which they are written for the Type statement.

DATA AVG/2./,IT/3/

The WATFOR and WATFIV FORTRAN compilers also permit implied DO loops in the DATA statement similar to the implied DO loops found in READ and WRITE statements. The following statement initializes A(1 to 5) and B(1 to 5) to zero, and A(6 to 10) and B(6 to 10) to one.

DATA (A(I),B(I),
I = 1,10)/10*0.,10*1./

Arrays can also be initialized. Values are assigned to arrays in column-major order with the left subscript varying most rapidly.

REAL A(2,3)/2*1.,2*2.,2*3./

A(1,1), A(2,1) set to 1
A(1,2), A(2,2) set to 2
A(1,3), A(2,3) set to 3

An iteration factor (n) can be appended to the value, causing it to be repeated n times. INIT((3)0) is the same as INIT(0,0,0).

DCL AVG INIT(2E0), IT INIT(3);

Arrays can also be initialized. Values are assigned to arrays in row-major order with the right subscript varying most rapidly.

DCL A(3,2) INIT((2)1E0,(2)2E0,
(2)3E0);

A(1,1), A(1,2) set to 1
A(2,1), A(2,2) set to 2
A(3,1), A(3,2) set to 3

The iteration factor applies to all values following it. An iteration factor of (1) can be used to terminate an iteration factor. INIT ((2)3,2,(1)6) is the same as INIT(3,2,3,2,6).

The iteration factor can be nested. In the following example, A is initialized to values of 2,3,2,3, 4,5,4,5, 6, 2,3,2,3, 4,5,4,5, 6.

DCL A(18) FIXED INIT ((2)((2)2,3,
(2)4,5,(1)6));

Except for STATIC storage described in the following section, the iteration factor can also be an arithmetic expression. INIT ((J*4)0) causes 24 values of zero to be generated if J has a value of 6.

INIT can specify a subroutine to be called to initialize the data (not allowed for STATIC data). In the following example, COMP is called as an internal procedure to assign values of 1 to 100 to array A.

```
DCL A(100) FIXED INIT CALL
                      COMP;
COMP: PROC;
        DO I = 1 TO 100;
        A(I) = I;
        END;
        END COMP;
```

Any arguments, including the name of the item to be initialized, can also be included in the subroutine call.

```
DCL A(2,3) FIXED INIT CALL
                   COMP(A,X,Z);
```

All rules for subroutine calls described in Chapter 8 apply. To call an external procedure, the data item must also be external, or be included as an argument in the call. The data name is known in internal procedures and does not have to be declared.

IV. ALLOCATION OF STORAGE

PL/I allocates storage for variables in three ways: as STATIC, AUTOMATIC, and CONTROLLED. All FORTRAN storage is STATIC, as is that for PL/I constants. STATIC storage is allocated when the program is loaded into core and remains intact during the entire run. It is generally the most efficient in execution time because the storage size is set during compilation and is allocated only once when the program is loaded into core. STATIC storage generally makes less efficient use of core storage because variables are allocated for the entire run even though they may be required for only a small portion of the run.

AUTOMATIC storage in PL/I is dynamically allocated upon each entry into a begin or procedure block within which the name is defined or first appears. (A block is a group of statements enclosed between a BEGIN;/END; or PROC;/END; pair. See Chapter 8 for a description of blocks.) The storage is released upon leaving the block, and any values stored in variables allocated within the block are lost. Arrays can have variable bounds because they are allocated during the execution of the program. AUTOMATIC storage makes efficient use of core storage by allocating and releasing storage as it is required by blocks, allowing the same storage to be reused by other blocks. But it takes computer time to allocate and release the storage. If a block containing AUTOMATIC storage lies within a loop, storage is allocated and released each time through the loop, and this can be costly. Note that AUTOMATIC storage allocated in the MAIN procedure has all the characteristics of STATIC storage, but requires execution time for allocation.

CONTROLLED storage is allocated and released by the execution of program statements. It has the same advantages and disadvantages as AUTOMATIC storage, but allows the programmer full control over the allocation. Remember that with dynamic storage allocation one must consider the maximum amount of storage required at one time in estimating the total size of the program. If it is not considered, a program could run for an hour, call a subroutine that allocates storage, and then terminate because the storage requested exceeds the amount available.

A. Static Storage

All data storage is allocated as static storage. The dimensions of arrays must be positive integers. In the following example, the array B and the variable I retain their values even after exit from the subroutine.

STATIC storage is specified in the DCL statement. The dimensions of static arrays must be decimal integer constants. In the following example, the array B and the variable I retain their values even after exit from the subroutine.

```
    SUBROUTINE COMP(A)
    REAL B(10)/10*0./

    I = 6
    RETURN
    END
```

```
COMP: PROC(A);
    DCL B(10) FLOAT STATIC
                   INIT((10)0E0);
    I = 6;
    RETURN;
    END COMP;
```

B. Automatic Storage

Not in FORTRAN.

Variables default to AUTOMATIC storage in PL/I, unless specifically declared to be STATIC, CONTROLLED, or EXTERNAL in the DCL statement. The dimensions of AUTOMATIC arrays can be any numeric expression, which is evaluated and truncated to integer in determining the bounds of the array. The expression is evaluated upon entry into the block, and is not affected by value changes within the block. In the following example, storage is allocated when the block is entered, and released upon exit from the block.

```
    X = 17.5E0;
    BEGIN;
    X = 10E0;
    DCL B(X); (Same as DCL B(17))
    END;
```

C. Controlled Storage

Not in FORTRAN.

CONTROLLED storage is allocated and released by execution of the ALLOCATE and FREE statements. CONTROLLED is usually abbreviated CTL. In the following example, A is allocated as an array when the ALLOCATE statement is executed, and the storage is released when the FREE statement is executed.

```
DCL A(10,20) FIXED(9) CTL;
ALLOCATE A;
FREE A;
```

The dimensions of CONTROLLED arrays can also be expressions. Dimensions in the ALLOCATE statement override those in the DCL statement. The number of dimensions must be specified in the DCL statement; either by assigning values, or using asterisks to indicate the number of dimensions. Attributes such as the data type, precision, and initial value can be specified in either the DCL or ALLOCATE statement. Those in the ALLOCATE statement override those in the DCL statement. In the following example, the dimensions of C are (5:8,10), and the dimension of D is (2).

```
DCL C(*,*) CTL, D(7) CTL;
I = 5;
ALLOCATE C(I:I+3,I*2) FLOAT(6)
            INIT(0), D(I/2) CHAR(3);
FREE B,D;
```

The ALLOCATION function determines whether storage for a CONTROLLED item has been allocated by returning a bit-string of '1'B if allocated, or '0'B if unallocated. In the following example, I equals '1'B if storage for A has been allocated.

```
I = ALLOCATION(A);
```

CONTROLLED storage can be allocated more than once and stacked in a *push-down, pop-up* list.

```
ALLOCATE I; (I is allocated)
I = 12; (I has the value 12)
ALLOCATE I; (I is allocated again and
now has no value. The value I = 12 is
pushed down in a list)
I = 20; (I has the value 20)
```

FREE I; (Storage for $I = 20$ is released, and the value $I = 12$ pops up to become the current value)

FREE I; (Storage for $I = 12$ is released, and I no longer exists)

V. SCOPE OF NAMES

All data names and statement labels within the main program or within subroutines, functions, or procedures are known only within that routine. The same name or label may be reused in other routines. Values in one routine can be passed to other subroutines as arguments in a subroutine call, or in common or external storage.

FORTRAN has no nested blocks or procedures.

Names defined in outer BEGIN or PROC blocks, described in Chapter 8, are known within inner nested blocks. Names defined within inner nested blocks are not known in outer blocks. Hence an inner block may use the same name as that in an outer block to represent a different item.

```
ONE:   PROC;
       DCL (A,B,C) FIXED;
START: B = 7; (B is set to 7)
TWO:   PROC;
       DCL (B,D) FIXED; (B and D are
       new variables. This B is not the
       same B defined above)
START: A = 6; (The A defined above is
       known in the inner block, and is
       set to 6. START can be reused as a
       label in an inner block)
       IF A = C THEN GO TO DONE;
       (The outer label DONE is known
       in the inner block)
       B = 12; (The inner B is set to 12)
       END TWO; (Storage for the inner
       B and D is released. At this point,
       A is equal to 6 and B equal to 7)
DONE:  END ONE; (Storage for the outer
       A and B is released)
```

VI. COMMON (EXTERNAL) STORAGE

Variables can be shared by several subroutines by naming them in a COMMON statement in each subroutine in which they

Variable names can be made known to several subroutines by declaring them EXTERNAL in the DCL statement in each

are used. The COMMON statement can also specify arrays.

COMMON A,B(100,10),C(3)

Common storage is often more convenient and more efficient than passing names as arguments in subroutine calls. The COMMON statement does not make the names known to the subroutines containing the COMMON statement. Instead it reserves a block of storage (called a *common block*) that is shared by all subroutines that contain the COMMON statement. For example, several subroutines containing the above COMMON statement could each refer to the variables A, B, or C.

Names are assigned to the common block in the order that they appear in the COMMON statement. Thus all of the names must appear in the same order in a COMMON statement in each subroutine that is to refer to common storage. Some computers operate more efficiently if the items in the COMMON statement are arranged in descending order of word length. The following example shows how common storage is allocated.

```
        SUBROUTINE SUB1
        COMMON A,B,C(2)
        END
        SUBROUTINE SUB2
        COMMON I(2),J,K,L
        END
        SUBROUTINE SUB3
        COMMON A,B,C(2)
        END
```

Storage is allocated in the order shown in the following table.

Position	SUB1	SUB2	SUB3
1	A	I(1)	A
2	B	I(2)	B
3	C(1)	J	C(1)
4	C(2)	K	C(2)
5	—	L	—

subroutine in which they are used. EXTERNAL can be abbreviated to EXT. (EXTERNAL names cannot be more than seven characters long for S/360/370.)

DCL A EXT, B(100,10) EXT, C(3)
EXT;

External storage is often more convenient and more efficient than passing names as arguments in subroutine calls. The EXT attribute makes the names known in all subroutines in which the names are declared with the EXT attribute. For example, several subroutines containing the above DCL statement could each refer to the variables A, B, or C.

The names need not appear in the same order in each DCL statement, and not all of the names need appear on each DCL statement. An external name must have the same attributes in each DCL statement. External names cannot be AUTOMATIC storage; STATIC is assumed if the EXT attribute is coded — unless the CONTROLLED attribute is specified.

The item named A in SUB1 and SUB3 is I(1) in SUB2, and changing the value of A in SUB1 or SUB3 changes the value of I(1) in SUB2. The above common block is called *blank common*, and it cannot be assigned initial values.

Labeled or *named common* is similar to blank common, but several labeled common areas may be established, each with separate names. Labeled common can also be assigned initial values. Labeled common is specified in the COMMON statement by preceding the data names with the labeled common name enclosed in slashes. In the following example, two labeled common areas named SET1 and SET2 are defined.

```
       SUBROUTINE SUB4
       COMMON /SET1/A,B,C
                     /SET2/D,E
       END
       SUBROUTINE SUB5
       COMMON /SET1/X(3)
       END
       SUBROUTINE SUB6
       COMMON /SET2/D,E
       END
```

The labeled common areas are stored as shown in the following table. Note that each labeled common area must have the same length in each COMMON statement.

Position	—SET1— SUB4	SUB5
1	A	X(1)
2	B	X(2)
3	C	X(3)

Position	—SET2— SUB4	SUB6
1	D	D
2	E	E

There can be several COMMON statements, and they are cumulative. The following two statements are the same as the third statement.

PL/I EXTERNAL storage is similar to labeled common. It can also be assigned initial values with the INIT attribute. Unlike labeled common, no common areas need be set up because the individual data names themselves are the labels. The same data names must be used wherever they appear.

```
COMMON A,B /SET3/D,E
              /SET4/F
COMMON X /SET5/Y
Same as:
COMMON A,B,X
         /SET3/D,E /SET4/F
                   /SET5/Y
```

Labeled common areas can be given initial values in a BLOCK DATA subprogram. There can be several BLOCK DATA subprograms, but data can be entered into a particular labeled common block by only one subprogram. The BLOCK DATA subprogram can contain only DIMENSION, COMMON, DATA, EQUIVALENCE, and Type statements. The following BLOCK DATA subprogram assigns A and I to the SET6 labeled common area, and C to the SET7 labeled common area. C is defined as integer, and all items are assigned initial values.

FORTRAN	PL/I
BLOCK DATA	DCL A(2) EXT INIT(2E0,0E0),
COMMON /SET6/A(2),	I EXT INIT(6),
I /SET7/C	
INTEGER C/0/	C EXT INIT(0E0);
DATA A/2.,0./,I/6/	
END	

VII. EQUIVALENCE (DEFINED) STORAGE

The EQUIVALENCE statement allows the same storage to be assigned different names. In the following example, A, B, and C all occupy the same storage location; so do D and E.

```
EQUIVALENCE (A,B,C),
            (D,E)
```

EQUIVALENCE allows data of one type to be stored in a variable of another data type without conversion. This is often needed for variables that contain character data. In the following example, the characters contained in J are stored in A without the conversion that would occur if A = J had been written.

The DEFINED attribute, abbreviated as DEF, in the DCL statement allows the same storage to be assigned different names. One variable is defined to overlay another. In the following example, A, B, and C all occupy the same storage location; so do D and E.

```
DCL A, B DEF A, C DEF A,
    D, E DEF D;
```

PL/I rules require that a defined item must be of the same data type and characteristics as the item to which it is defined, but data of one type can in practice be defined to another data type, and at present the only bad side effect is a warning diagnostic message. In the following example, the characters contained in J are stored in A without the conversion that would occur if $A = J$; had been written.

```
DATA J/4HTEST/            DCL J CHAR(4) INIT('TEST');
EQUIVALENCE (A,I)         DCL A, I CHAR(4) DEF A;
I = J                     I = J;
```

The UNSPEC function described in Chapter 5 is a better way to do the above. The statement would be written as follows.

UNSPEC(A) = UNSPEC(J);

An item cannot be defined to a defined item.

DCL A, B DEF A, C DEF B; Wrong!

Items in an EQUIVALENCE statement can be given initial values. The results are unpredictable if both items made equivalent to each other are given initial values. Items in an EQUIVALENCE statement can also appear in a COMMON statement.

A defined item cannot be given an initial value or be given the EXTERNAL attribute, but the item to which it is defined can be given an initial value and can have the EXTERNAL attribute.

```
DATA A/0./                DCL A EXT INIT(0E0),
COMMON A                       B DEF A;
EQUIVALENCE (A,B)
```

Arrays can also be defined to occupy the same storage.

Arrays can also be defined to occupy the same storage.

```
DIMENSION A(100,100),     DCL A(100,100),
          B(100,100)
EQUIVALENCE (A(1,1),            B(100,100) DEF A;
            B(1,1))
```

The name iSUB, in which i has values from 1 to n where n is the number of dimensions of the array, is a special PL/I variable name used in a defined array. The iSUB coded in the defined array assumes the range from the lower to upper bounds of dimension n of the array to which it is defined. This aids in defining one array on top of another.

```
DCL A(10,20:30),
       B(10,10) DEF A(1SUB,2SUB);
B(1,1) is A(1,20), B(1,2) is A(1,21),...,
B(10,10) is A(10,30).
```

An array can be redefined to be several arrays.

An array can be redefined to be several arrays.

```
DIMENSION A(100),B(50),   DCL A(100),
          C(50)
```

<table>
<tr><td>

EQUIVALENCE (A(1),B(1)),
                   (A(51),C(1))
B(1 to 50) is A(1 to 50),
C(1 to 50) is A(51 to 100)

</td><td>

B(50) DEF A(1SUB),
       C(50) DEF A(1SUB + 50);
B(1 to 50) is A(1 to 50),
C(1 to 50) is A(51 to 100)

</td></tr>
</table>

The dimensions of arrays need not be the same. The arrays are made equivalent in the order in which the elements are stored in core.

The rule is that arrays should have the same number of dimensions. They need not, however, although a warning diagnostic message will result. The arrays are made equivalent in the order in which the elements are stored in core.

DIMENSION A(20,10),
                   B(200)
EQUIVALENCE (A,B)

DCL A(20,10),

       B(200) DEF A(1SUB,2SUB);

Arrays can be effectively stored in column-major order by redefining an array. In the following example, array B is stored in column-major order.

DCL A(2,3),
       B(3,2) DEF A(2SUB,1SUB);
A(1,1) is B(1,1)
A(1,2) is B(2,1)
A(1,3) is B(3,1)
A(2,1) is B(1,2)
A(2,2) is B(2,2)
A(2,3) is B(3,2)

The DEFINED item may be a structure if it is level 1. Most compilers do not permit arrays to be DEFINED within structures. The DEFINED attribute cannot be used for a VARYING string, or assigned to a VARYING string.

Bit- and character-fixed-length strings can be redefined into separate strings by the POSITION attribute. The abbreviation is POS. POS(1) is assumed if omitted. The defined variables cannot extend beyond the item to which they are defined.

DCL A CHAR(50),
       B CHAR(10) DEF A,
       C CHAR(10) DEF A POS(11),
       D CHAR(30) DEF A POS(21);
B(1 to 10) is A(1 to 10)
C(1 to 10) is A(11 to 20)
D(1 to 30) is A(21 to 50)

VIII. EXERCISES

1. Define a floating-point array named SIZE with 100 elements and fill it to values from 1 to 100.

2. Write the data declarations necessary to define variables as given below.

• Names beginning with W through Z are to be integer.	• The names W, WAY, and XERO are to be fixed decimal with sufficient precision to contain the number 9999.99999.
• The names TAX, FIRST, and ONLY are to be logical.	• The names TAX, FIRST, and ONLY are to contain character-strings of lengths up to 115 characters.
• Names beginning with K and N are to be single-precision floating-point.	• The names KLEIN, NOT, and IT are to be single-precision floating-point.
• The names KOST, WEIGHT, and ZERO are to be double precision.	• The names KOST, WEIGHT, and ZERO are to be double precision.
• The names AREA and YOST are to be complex.	• The names AREA and YOST are to be complex.

3. Define an integer array named SIZE to contain the population of each of 10 precincts within each city, 3 cities within each county, 30 counties within each state, and 50 states. What is the size of the array? Write the necessary statements to sum the total for all states.

4. What will the array A contain after the following statements are executed?

```
              INTEGER A(5,2)/4*3,3*2/      I, J = 3;
              A = 7                        DCL A(5,2) FIXED INIT((I)3,(J)2);
              DO 100 K = 2, 5, 3           A(2,*) = 7;
    100       A(K,1) = K                   DO K = 5 TO 1 BY −I;
                                           A(K,1) = K;
                                           END;
```

5. Two arrays, one integer, and one floating-point, must be defined. The integer array is named SIZE and must have dimensions of (1000,20). The floating-point array is named MAX and has dimensions of (500,20). The arrays are not used at the same time, and together they are too large to be contained on the computer. Write the statements necessary to overlay one array upon the other. In addition, for PL/I accomplish the same results by allocating the arrays dynamically.

6. A single-dimension integer array named IVAL contains 100 elements. Sort the values of the array into ascending numerical order, with the smallest value in IVAL(1) and the largest value in IVAL(100).

7. The variables XTRA, INT, and TOTAL must be defined to be double precision. An integer array named MAX of dimensions (100,50) must also be defined. These data items are to be shared by several subroutines. Write the necessary declarative statements.

8. Define a single-dimension floating-point array named CITY with 90 elements. Then define three arrays to overlay CITY; TOWN elements 1 to 30, BERG elements 31 to 60, and HAMLET elements 61 to 90.

9. Define a floating-point array named SIZE with 100 elements and fill it with zeros. Use a BLOCK DATA subprogram in FORTRAN, and a subroutine call in the INIT attribute in PL/I.

10. Define two floating-point arrays named ACCEL and MASS with dimensions (50,20). Multiply the corresponding elements of each array together and store the results in an integer array named FORCE that has the same dimensions.

Chapter 8

Program Organization

I. STATEMENT GROUPINGS

FORTRAN does not have statement groupings. PL/I has three types of statement groupings: the DO-group, begin blocks, and procedure blocks. The *DO-group* allows several statements to be placed in the THEN or ELSE clauses of an IF statement. The *begin block* also encloses a group of statements, and in addition allocates automatic storage and limits the scope of names and labels. The *procedure block* is like the begin block, but it is invoked by the CALL statement rather than being executed in sequence.

A. DO-groups

FORTRAN

PL/I

Not in FORTRAN.

DO-groups consist of statements enclosed between a DO; and END; pair, and may be placed wherever a single statement may go. They are executed as if the DO; and END; were not there. The following example shows the use of a DO-group in an IF statement.

```
IF A = B THEN DO;
                I = 1;
                J = K*2;
                END;
        ELSE  DO; I = 2;
                J = 0;
                END;
```

B. Begin blocks

Not in FORTRAN.

A begin block is a group of statements enclosed between a BEGIN; and END; pair. Begin blocks are executed in sequence like single statements, and must be entered at the BEGIN statement. Exit can be made from a block by reaching the END statement, or by the GO TO statement. The following is an example of a begin block, and all of the statements are executed in sequence.

```
A = 3;
BEGIN;
DCL B;
B = A; A = A*3 + B;
END;
```

Names defined within a block are known only within the block, but names defined in an outer block are also known within the inner block. Automatic storage is allocated when a block is entered, and the storage is released upon exit from the block. The scope of names and storage allocation are described in Chapter 7.

Begin blocks are primarily used in conjunction with the ON condition described in Chapter 11, and in limiting the scope of names.

C.   Procedure Blocks

Not in FORTRAN.

A procedure block is a group of statements enclosed between a *'label*: PROCEDURE;' 'END *label*;' pair. (PROCEDURE is usually written in its short form as PROC.) The scope of names and allocation of storage is like that of begin blocks. Procedure blocks differ from begin blocks in that they are not executed in sequence, but must be invoked by the CALL statement. Processing skips around procedure blocks if they are encountered during execution. The following example shows how procedure blocks are written and invoked, and the actual sequence of execution.

As written: As executed:
    B = A + 1;   B = A + 1;
    SAVE: PROC;   B = 0;
        A = B;   A = B;
    END SAVE;   X = B + A;
    B = 0;
    CALL SAVE;
    X = B + A;

II.   MAIN PROGRAM

The main program begins with the first FORTRAN statement, and ends with the END statement. (The END statement is not executable, and does not stop execution.) The STOP statement terminates execution, and it can be executed at any point in the

The main program begins with a *'name*: PROC OPTIONS(MAIN);' statement, and ends with the 'END *name*;' statement. (S/360/370 program names are limited to seven characters in length.) Execution is terminated by executing the final END main program or in a subroutine. (A 'CALL EXIT' statement, a carry over from older FORTRAN compilers, is sometimes used, and is equivalent to the STOP statement.)

statement of the main program, by executing the RETURN statement anywhere within the main program, or by executing the STOP statement anywhere within the main program or in a subroutine. The RETURN statement is the normal way of terminating execution. STOP is for abnormal termination, and prints a message to the operator in S/360/370.

```
          statements
          STOP
          perhaps more statements
          END
```

```
name: PROC OPTIONS(MAIN);
          statements;
          RETURN;
          perhaps more statements;
          END name;
```

S/360/370 FORTRAN allows a return code ranging from zero to 4095 to be set by the STOP statement and tested by subsequent job steps. The general form is STOP *n*, where *n* is an integer constant or variable.

S/360/370 PL/I allows a return code ranging from zero to 4095 to be set by the IHESARC library subroutine. The following statements are required to invoke it.

```
          STOP 16
```

```
          DCL IHESARC ENTRY(FIXED
                              BIN(31));
          CALL IHESARC(expression);
```

III. FUNCTIONS

A function operates on the arguments in a function reference, and returns a single value. Function references may appear in any expression. The rules for arguments in functions are the same as those for subroutines described in the next section.

A. External Functions

External functions begin with the FUNCTION statement and end with the END statement. The RETURN statement, of which there may be several, returns control to the invoking program. Each external function can be compiled separately.

External functions begin with a PROC statement and end with an END statement. (System 360/370 limits external procedure names to seven characters in length.) The RETURN statement, of which there may be several, returns control to the invoking program. Each external function can be compiled separately.

The function value is returned by the function name appearing on the left side of an assignment statement within the function. Only single element values can be returned.

The function value is returned by the RETURN statement within the function in the form of RETURN(*expression*). Only single element values can be returned.

```
        FUNCTION DIV(A,B)          DIV: PROC(A,B);
        IF (A.EQ.0.) GO TO 100        IF B = ·0E0 THEN RETURN(0E0);
        DIV = A/B                         ELSE RETURN (A/B);
        RETURN                     END DIV;
100     DIV = 0.
        RETURN
        END
```

The above function returns a value of zero if B equals zero; otherwise it returns A/B. In the following statement, DIV(17.3,X) is invoked, and the value of zero or 17.3/X participates in the expression.

$$A = W*C*DIV(17.3,X) \qquad\qquad A = W*C*DIV(17.3E0,X);$$

The data type returned by the function must be declared explicitly if other than the default (I to N, integer; all else floating-point) based on the first character of the name is desired.

The data type is specified by preceding the FUNCTION statement with the data type, INTEGER, REAL, LOGICAL, COMPLEX, or DOUBLE PRECISION.

The data type is specified by adding the RETURNS(*type*) attribute to the PROC statement, where *type* is the data type to be returned (FIXED, FLOAT, FIXED BIN, CHAR, or BIT).

```
        INTEGER FUNCTION          EXP: PROC(I,J) RETURNS(FIXED
                    EXP(I,J)                            BIN(31));
        EXP = I**J                    RETURN(I**J);
        RETURN                    END EXP;
        END
```

A Type statement in the invoking program must also describe the function type if the default based on the first character of the function name is overridden. The following is required to invoke the above function.

A RETURNS(*type*) attribute in a DCL statement must also be included in the invoking program if the default based on the first character of the function name is overridden. The following is required to invoke the above function.

```
        INTEGER EXP               DCL EXP RETURNS(FIXED
                                                    BIN(31));
        I = EXP(N,M)              I = EXP(N,M);
```

FORTRAN functions must have at least one argument, even if it is not used.

PL/I functions may have no arguments.

B.   Internal Functions

FORTRAN provides a special one-statement function definition within a subprogram. The general form is:

$$name(dummy\text{-}arguments) = $$
$$expression$$

PL/I functions and subroutines can be internal procedures, and can be placed anywhere within a program; execution passes around them. The rules for internal functions and subroutines are the same as for external functions.

The *name* is the function name; there must be one or more *dummy arguments* in the list; the same argument cannot appear more than once; and the *expression* evaluates the function. Array names cannot appear in the argument list or in the expression. The function definitions must be the first statements in the subprogram. The *dummy-argument* names can also be used as normal variables within the subprogram.

FORTRAN	PL/I

HOURS(HR,AM,SC) =
  HR + AM/60. + SC/3600.
	HOURS: PROC(HR,AM,SC);
	  RETURN(HR + AM/60E0 +
	       SC/3600E0);
	END HOURS;

DIST = RATE*HOURS(A, B,C)	DIST = RATE*HOURS(A,B,C);

(Same as:)
DIST = RATE*(A + B/60. +
       C/3600.)
	(Same as:)
	DIST = RATE*(A + B/60E0 + C/
	       3600E0);

C. Function References

Function references are normally recognized by their form, *name(arguments)*, and the context within which they are used.

FORTRAN functions must have at least one argument, even if it is not used, to enable FORTRAN to distinguish the function reference from a variable name. The following function is given a dummy argument so that it will not be treated as a variable.

PL/I functions need not have arguments, as they can be specifically declared to be functions with the ENTRY attribute in the DCL statement within the program invoking the function. (The RETURNS attribute will also accomplish this.)

DCL PI ENTRY; (or DCL PI
            RETURNS(FLOAT(6));)

FORTRAN	PL/I
D = PI(0)*R**2	D = PI*R**2;
FUNCTION PI(A) PI = 3.1416 RETURN END	PI: PROC RETURNS(FLOAT); RETURN(3.1416E0); END PI;

If an array and a function have the same name, all references to the name are to the array and not to the function. For example, if an array and a function are both named SIZE, a statement such as Y = SIZE(4) stores the fourth element of array SIZE in Y rather than the value of the function SIZE with an argument of 4.

If a data item declared in the DCL statement and a function have the same name, all references to the name are to the data item and not to the function. For example, if an array and a function are both named SIZE, a statement such as Y = SIZE(4); stores the fourth element of array SIZE in Y rather than the value of the function SIZE with an argument of 4.

PL/I provides the BUILTIN attribute to overcome the problem of distinguishing variable names from function references. BUILTIN causes all references within the scope of the DCL statement within which it appears to be function references. In the following example, SQRT is defined as an array, and is redefined as a function reference in an internal block with the BUILTIN attribute.

```
DCL SQRT(10);
A = SQRT(4); (Element 4 of SQRT
                               array)
BEGIN;
DCL SQRT BUILTIN;
A = SQRT(4); (SQRT function
                          invoked)
END;
A = SQRT(4); (Element 4 of SQRT
                               array)
```

IV. SUBROUTINES

Subroutines consist of a collection of self-contained statements that can be compiled separately from other parts of the program. They begin with the SUBROUTINE statement in FORTRAN and the PROC statement in PL/I, and end with the END statement. Subroutines are invoked by the CALL statement. The RETURN statement, which can appear several times within the subroutine, returns control to the calling program at the statement following the CALL statement. (The PL/I END statement also acts as a RETURN statement if it is executed.) Names and labels defined within a subroutine are known only within that subroutine, and these names may be used in the main program or other subroutines for other purposes. Subroutine names cannot be longer than seven characters in System 360/370. The following example illustrates a CALL statement to a subroutine named TIME.

```
CALL TIME                     CALL TIME;
  ___                           ___

SUBROUTINE TIME               TIME: PROC;
statements                      statements;
RETURN                          RETURN;
perhaps more statements         perhaps more statements;
END                           END TIME;
```

A. Subroutine and Function Arguments

Subroutines and functions are passed data either by COMMON or EXTERNAL storage as described in Chapter 7, or by arguments in the CALL statement. The CALL statement or function reference can contain a list of variables, constants, or expressions as *arguments*. The arguments are associated one-to-one with a corresponding list of names in the SUB-ROUTINE, FUNCTION, or PROC statement. The argument list in the CALL or function reference and the list of names in the receiving subroutine or function must contain the same number of items in the same order, and be of the same data type. The subroutine or function is given access to the arguments, and it can change the value of the arguments upon return. The following example illustrates a CALL statement with four arguments.

CALL SUBS(A,B,C,D)

CALL SUBS(A,B,C,D);

The names in the SUBROUTINE, FUNCTION, or PROC statement can be different from those passed to it by the CALL or function reference. These names are called *dummy variables* in FORTRAN and *parameters* in PL/I. In the following statement, the A in the CALL above is associated with A1, B with A2, C with A3, and D with A4.

SUBROUTINE SUBS(A1,
                A2,A3,A4)

SUBS: PROC(A1,A2,A3,A4);

FORTRAN subroutines must have at least one argument, even if it is not used.	PL/I subroutines may have no arguments.
The values of the arguments in the CALL or function reference are stored in the dummy variables upon entry to the subroutine or function, and the values are stored back in the arguments upon RETURN. This is termed *call-by-value*, and is illustrated in the following example.	The names of the arguments in the CALL or function reference replace the names in the PROC list upon entry to the subroutine or function. Hence the subroutine operates upon the actual arguments. This is termed *call-by-name*, and is illustrated in the following example.

X = 3.
CALL SUB(X,X)
—

SUBROUTINE SUB(A,B)
(The value 3 is stored in A and B.)
A = 2. (A set to 2)
B = B + A (B = 3 + 2 = 5)
RETURN
(A is stored in X and then B is stored in X. X contains 5.)
END

X = 3E0;
CAL SUB(X,X);
—

SUB: PROC(A,B);
(The name of X replaces the names of A and B.)
A = 2E0; (X set to 2)
B = B + A; (X = 2 + 2 = 4)
RETURN;
(X contains 4)

END SUB;

Some FORTRAN compilers allow call-by-name to be specified by enclosing the dummy arguments between slashes in the SUB-ROUTINE or FUNCTION statement.

SUBROUTINE SUB(/A/,
                B,/C/)

If a literal is passed to a subroutine or function as an argument, care must be taken that the value is not changed. In the following example, the value of the literal '2.' is changed to '4.' with possible disastrous results that are extremely difficult to detect.

If an argument in a CALL or function reference has no name, as for literals and expressions, the value is stored in a dummy variable in the subroutine or function (call-by-value). Unlike FORTRAN, the values are not stored back in the list of arguments upon exit from the subroutine or function for call-by-value. The following example illustrates this.

```
CALL TEST(2.)
B = 2. + 2. (B is set to 8.)
      ___
SUBROUTINE TEST(A)
A = 4. (A is set to 4.)
RETURN (A is stored back
                    in 2.)
END
```

```
CALL TEST(2E0);
B = 2E0 + 2E0; (B is set to 4.)
      ___
TEST: PROC(A);
    A = 4E0; (A is set to 4.)
    RETURN; (A is not stored back
                    in 2E0)
END TEST;
```

All dummy variables and parameters must be explicitly declared to be the proper data type if other than the default (I to N integer; all else floating-point) based on the first character of the name is desired. In the following example, both A and C require explicit definitions, but B defaults properly.

```
CALL MATCH(I,X,J)
      ___
SUBROUTINE
          MATCH(A,B,C)
INTEGER A,C
```

```
CALL MATCH(I,X,J);
      ___
MATCH: PROC(A,B,C);

      DCL (A,C) FIXED
                    BIN(31);
```

The data type of the arguments that a procedure expects can be declared in the calling program in a DCL statement with the ENTRY attribute. PL/I will then automatically convert the arguments to the required data types, if necessary, and store them in dummy variables for call-by-value. The value of the arguments in the calling program then can be changed. The following example illustrates the ENTRY attribute.

```
DCL RIGHT ENTRY(FIXED(3),
                    FLOAT(6));
CALL RIGHT(A,Z); (A is converted to
fixed and Z to float if they are not of
these data types.)
```

Be especially careful to use ENTRY to declare the data type in the calling program when using literals in calls. For example, the precision of decimal fixed-point literals depends on the number; that is, 7.6 has precision (2,1) and 164.33 has precision (5,2). Thus a subroutine written to accept the number 7.6 with precision (2,1) will give a data exception if called with a literal of 126.33 having a precision of (5,2). Declaring the precision with the ENTRY attribute causes the literal to be stored in a dummy variable, and the called subroutine can declare the parameter to have the same precision.

```
DCL SUB ENTRY(FIXED(10,3),
                        CHAR(50));
CALL SUB(2,'THIS WAY');
CALL SUB(1001.32,'LONG
                    ARGUMENT');

        —

SUB: PROC(A,B);
        DCL A FIXED(10,3),
                    B CHAR(50);
```

Indicate the presence of an argument whose precision does not need to be defined with the ENTRY attribute by a comma.

```
DCL SUB ENTRY(,CHAR(6),,
                    FIXED(8),);
CALL SUB(A,'IT',B,2,C);

        —

SUB: PROC(V,W,X,Y,Z);
        DCL W CHAR(6),
                    Y FIXED(8);
```

Some FORTRAN compilers permit statement labels to be passed as subroutine (but not function) arguments. The RETURN n statement returns to the nth statement label, where n is an integer constant or variable. The SUBROUTINE statement must denote the dummy arguments containing labels with asterisks. The statement labels in the CALL statement must be preceded by the & sign.

PL/I permits statement labels and label variables to be passed as subroutine and function arguments. The parameters must be defined as LABEL within the procedure. A GO TO statement within the procedure may transfer directly to the label.

FORTRAN	PL/I
CALL SUB(A,B,&100,C, &200,&300) (The 3rd, 5th, and 6th arguments are statement labels.)	CALL SUB(A,B,S100,C,S200,S300); (The 3rd, 5th, and 6th arguments are statement labels.)
SUBROUTINE SUB(X,Y,*, Z,*,*) (The dummy arguments containing statement labels are indicated by the asterisks.)	SUB: PROC(X,Y,L1,Z,L2,L3); DCL (L1,L2,L3) LABEL;
RETURN (Normal return to statement following the call.)	RETURN; (Normal return to statement following the call.)
RETURN 1 (Return to statement 100.)	GO TO L1; (Return to statement S100.)
RETURN 2 (Return to statement 200.)	GO TO L2; (Return to statement S200.)
RETURN 3 (Return to statement 300.)	GO TO L3; (Return to statement S300.)

B. Arrays as Arguments

Arrays (and string variables in PL/I) must also be declared in the subroutine or function if they are passed as arguments. The array size and dimensions (or string length) must match those in the invoking program. Arrays are call-by-name in both FORTRAN and PL/I.

FORTRAN	PL/I
DIMENSION A(10,2), I(6) CALL CHECK(A,I)	DCL A(10,2), I CHAR(24); CALL CHECK(A,I);
—	—
SUBROUTINE CHECK(X,K) DIMENSION X(10,2), K(6)	CHECK: PROC(X,K); DCL X(10,2), K CHAR(24);

The dimension of arrays (and string length in PL/I) can also be passed as arguments in the CALL or function reference, providing adjustable dimension sizes within subroutines and functions.

FORTRAN	PL/I
INTEGER A(10,2) DIMENSION I(6)	DCL A(10,2) FIXED BIN(31), I CHAR(24); DCL CHECK ENTRY(,FIXED(5), FIXED(5),,FIXED(5));
CALL CHECK(A,10,2,I,6)	CALL CHECK(A,10,2,I,24);
—	—
SUBROUTINE CHECK(X,I,J,K,L) FLOAT X(I.J) DIMENSION K(L)	CHECK: PROC(X,I,J,K,L); DCL X(I,J) FLOAT, (I,J,L) FIXED (5), K CHAR(L);

The dimensions of arrays and string lengths can be declared in subroutines and functions with asterisks, and the size of the current argument in the invoking program is used in the DCL statement.

FOCUS: PROC(X);
      DCL X(*);
      ___

DCL A(10), B(100);
CALL FOCUS(X); (DCL X(10);
                in FOCUS)
CALL FOCUS(B); (DCL X(100);
                in FOCUS)

C. Subroutine and Function Names as Arguments

Subroutine and function names themselves can be passed as arguments in calls to other subroutines or functions.

The names must be declared in an EXTERNAL statement in the invoking program so that FORTRAN will know it is not the name of a variable. The EXTERNAL statement must precede any executable statements in the program. The following example passes a subroutine name as an argument in a function reference.

EXTERNAL SUB1
A = FAST(SUB1,2,3)
___

FUNCTION FAST(A,I,J)
CALL A(I,J) (Same as CALL
            SUB1(I,J))

The names must be declared with an ENTRY attribute in the DCL statement so that PL/I will know that it is not the name of a variable. The following example passes a subroutine name as an argument in a function reference.

DCL SUB1 ENTRY;
A = FAST(SUB1,2,3);
___

FAST: PROC(A,I,J);
      CALL A(I,J); (Same as CALL SUB1
                (I,J);)

If a function has no arguments, PL/I must be told when it is to pass the function name as an argument, and when it is to evaluate the function and pass the value as an argument. The function is evaluated if the name is enclosed in parenthesis in the argument list.

CALL NEXT(RANDOM); (The name of RANDOM is passed.)
CALL NEXT((RANDOM)); (The value returned by RANDOM is passed.)

D. Multiple Entry Points

Subroutines and functions can have multiple entry points specified by the ENTRY statement within the subroutine or function. The ENTRY statement can also list dummy arguments, which can differ from those in the SUBROUTINE, FUNCTION, or PROC statement in number, order, and type.

SUBROUTINE	FLOAT: PROC(A,C);
FLOAT(A,C)	
GO TO 100	GO TO S100;
ENTRY FIX(B,C,I)	FIX: ENTRY(B,C,I);
INTEGER B	DCL B FIXED;
A = B + I	A = B + I;
100 C = C + A	S100: C = C + A;
RETURN	RETURN;
END	END FLOAT;

CALL FLOAT(2.,VALUE)	CALL FLOAT(2E0,VALUE);
CALL FIX(2,VALUE,17)	CALL FIX(2,VALUE,17);

Control passes through an ENTRY statement· and as a result it is often preceded with a RETURN or GO TO statement as shown above. The ENTRY name of a function can be of a different data type than the function itself. It either defaults according to the first character of the entry name, or is specified by the Type statement in FORTRAN or the RETURNS option in PL/I.

REAL FUNCTION	FLOAT: PROC(A) RETURNS(FLOAT);
FLOAT(A)	
FLOAT = A**A	RETURN(A**A);
RETURN	FIX: ENTRY(A) RETURNS(FIXED);
ENTRY FIX(A)	RETURN(A**A);
INTEGER FIX	END FLOAT;
FIX = A**A	
RETURN	
END	

A = FLOAT(17.)	A = FLOAT(17E0);
I = FIX(17)	I = FIX(17);

The GENERIC statement allows a reference to a single name to result in selecting one of several entry names to be invoked, based on the data type of the arguments in the reference. In the following example, the generic name TIME has two arguments, and FTIME is called if the arguments are floating-point, and DTIME is called if the arguments are fixed decimal.

```
DCL TIME GENERIC (FTIME
         ENTRY(FLOAT,FLOAT),
         DTIME(FIXED,FIXED));
CALL  TIME(2E0,7E0);  (Same  as
    CALL FTIME(2E0,7E0);)
CALL  TIME(2,7);  (Same  as  CALL
    DTIME(2,7);)
```

E.   Compilation of Subroutine and Functions

External subroutines and functions may be compiled separately from the main program and other subroutines and functions. Thus a change in a single subroutine or function does not require recompilation of the entire program. Considerable compilation time can be saved by breaking up large programs into several external subroutines and functions. The COMMON statement in FORTRAN and the EXTERNAL attribute in PL/I permit data to be shared without having to include the data as arguments in the subroutine call or function reference. S/360/370 PL/I requires a special PROCESS control statement to precede each external subroutine and function in a single compilation. FORTRAN generally does not require any special control statements.

Job card and system control statements	*Job card and system control statements*
main program	*name*: **PROC OPTIONS(MAIN)**;
program statements	*program statements*
	any internal subroutines or functions
END	**END** *name*;
	***PROCESS** (* in column 1)
subroutines or functions	*external subroutine or function*
⋮	***PROCESS**
	external subroutine or function
	⋮
System control statements, data, etc.	*System control statements, data, etc.*

V.   EXERCISES

1.   Write a subroutine named RECTNG that computes and returns the area of a rectangle, given its length and width as arguments. Show how the subroutine would be called.

2.   Write a function named AREA to do the same as in Exercise 1. What are the advantages of such a function over the subroutine? What is the main limitation of functions? Show how the function would be invoked.

3.   Write a subroutine named ARRAY to store the product of the array indicies of a two-dimensional array (i.e., element (1,1) set to 1*1, element (1,2) set to 1*2, etc.). Write the subroutine such that it can accommodate arrays of any size. Show how the subroutine would be called.

4. Write a single floating-point function named **METER** to convert distances into meters. The function is to convert units of inches, feet, yards, and miles. (1 inch = 0.0254 meters, 1 mile = 1609.35 meters.) Use a separate entry point within the function for each unit. Show how the function would be invoked.

5. Write a function named **MINI** to return the smallest value in an n by m floating-point array.

6. Write a subroutine named **SET** that searches a single-dimensional integer array of any size and sets negative values to −1, positive values to +1, and leaves zero values undisturbed.

7. A single-dimension floating-point array named **TAX** appears in several arithmetic expressions within a program. It does not appear on the left-hand side of an assignment statement. It is desired that each instance of the TAX array assume a value of 100 within the arithmetic expressions. Assume that the declarative statement for TAX is removed. Write an internal function to set references to the TAX array to a value of 100. For example, the statement A = TAX(20) would store the value 100 into A.

Chapter 9

Built-in Functions

The following built-in functions are provided as a part of the language. However, not all compilers will have all of the following functions.

FORTRAN

Separate FORTRAN functions are required for each numeric data type. The first character of the name usually specifies the data type: I to N for integer, D for double-precision, C for complex, and the remaining for real floating-point.

Arguments in function references may be constants, variables, or expressions.

Functions cannot operate upon arrays, but only upon single elements of arrays.

$$\text{DIMENSION A(2), B(2)}$$
$$\text{B = SQRT(A)}$$
Same as:
$$\text{B(1) = SQRT(A(1))}$$

PL/I

A single PL/I function operates on all data types.

Arguments in function references may be constants, variables, or expressions.

Functions can operate on arrays. The function operates upon each element of the array, and returns an array of results of the same dimensions as the argument.

$$\text{DCL A(2), B(2);}$$
$$\text{B = SQRT(A);}$$
Same as:
$$\text{B(1) = SQRT(A(1));}$$
$$\text{B(2) = SQRT(A(2));}$$

I. ARITHMETIC FUNCTIONS

1. ABS, Absolute value. Return the absolute value of the argument. For example, ABS(-25.6) yields 25.6, ABS(25.6) yields 25.6.

IABS(*integer*) yields integer
ABS(*real*) yields real
DABS(*dbl*) yields double†
CABS(*complex*) yields real

ABS(*expression*)

2. BINARY, Convert a decimal number to a binary fixed-point number. Converts the decimal expression to a binary fixed-point number of precision (w,d).

Not in FORTRAN

BINARY(*decimal-expression,w,d*);

† *dbl* and *double* are used to abbreviate double-precision floating-point.

3.   CEIL, Ceiling. Return the smallest integer greater than or equal to the argument. For example, CEIL(-5.3) yields -5.0, CEIL(5.3) yields 6.0.

No equivalent function; use following state-   CEIL(*expression*)   (not complex)
ments.

        ICEIL $=$ *real*
        A $=$ *real* $-$ ICEIL
        IF (A.GT.0.)
                ICEIL $=$ ICEIL $+$ 1

4.   CMPLX/COMPLEX, Convert two numbers to complex.

CMPLX(*real,real*) yields complex   COMPLEX(*expression,expression*)
                                                        yields complex

DCMPLX(*dbl,dbl*) yields dbl complex

                                                COMPLEX may also be used as a pseudo-
                                                variable to assign the real and imaginary
                                                parts of a complex number to two variables.

                                                COMPLEX(*var1,var2*) $=$ *complex*;
                                                        The real part is stored in *var1*, and the
                                                        imaginary part in *var2*.

5.   CONJG, Obtain the conjugate of a complex number.

CONJG(*real,real*) yields complex   CONJG(*expression,expression*)
                                                        yields complex

DCONJG(*dbl,dbl*) yields dbl complex

6.   DBLE/FLOAT, Convert number to double-precision floating-point. Converts the argument to double-precision floating-point by extending the number with zeros.

DBLE(*real*) yields double   FLOAT(*float*,16) yields FLOAT(16)

7.   DECIMAL, Convert a binary number to a decimal number. Converts the binary expression to a decimal number of precision (*w,d*).

Not in FORTRAN.   DECIMAL(*binary-expression,w,d*)

8.   DIM, Positive difference. DIM(*a,b*) yields the maximum of zero or (*a − b*). For example, DIM(− 2.,5.) yields 0., DIM(5.,− 2.) yields 7.0, DIM(5.0,10.0) yields 0.

IDIM(*integer,integer*) yields integer
DIM(*real,real*) yields real
DDIM(*dbl,dbl*) yields double

No equivalent function; use following expression.
$$DIM = MAX(0,A − B);$$

9.   FLOAT, Convert number to floating-point. Converts argument to single-precision floating-point.

FLOAT(*integer*) yields real

FLOAT(*expression*,6) yields
FLOAT(6)

10.   FLOOR. Return largest integer that is less than or equal to the argument. For example, FLOOR(− 5.3) yields − 6.0, FLOOR(5.3) yields 5.0.

No equivalent function; use following statements.

```
     IFLOOR = real
     A = real − IFLOOR
     IF (A.LT.0.)
        IFLOOR = IFLOOR − 1
```

FLOOR(*expression*)   (not complex)

11.   IMAG, Find the imaginary part of a complex number.

AIMAG(*complex*) yields real
DIMAG(*dbl-complex*) yields double

IMAG(*complex*)

IMAG may also be used as a pseudovariable to assign a real number or the real part of a complex number to the imaginary part of a complex number.

IMAG(*complex*) = *value*;

12.   IFIX/FIXED, Convert number to integer. Truncates argument to integer.

IFIX(*real*) yields integer

FIXED(*expression*) yields FIXED DEC if argument is DEC, or FIXED BIN if argument is BIN.

13. INT/TRUNC, Truncate a floating-point number. The argument is truncated at the decimal point. For example, -3.9 becomes -3.0, 3.9 becomes 3.0.

INT(*real*) yields integer   TRUNC(*expression*)   (not complex)
IDINT(*dbl*) yields integer
AINT(*real*) yields real
DINT(*dbl*) yields double

14. MAX, Find the maximum argument. Return the maximum value of a list of arguments. For example, MAX($-100,5,1$) yields 5.

MAX0(*int,int,...*) yields integer   MAX(*expression,expression,...*)
AMAX0(*int,int,...*) yields real   (not complex)
MAX1(*real,real,...*) yields integer
AMAX1(*real,real,...*) yields real
DMAX1(*dbl,dbl,...*) yields double

15. MIN, Find the minimum argument. Return the minimum value of a list of arguments. For example, MIN($-3,5,0$) yields -3.

MIN0(*int,int,...*) yields integer   MIN(*expression,expression,...*)
AMIN0(*int,int,...*) yields real   (not complex)
MIN1(*real,real,...*) yields integer
AMIN1(*real,real,...*) yields real
DMIN1(*dbl,dbl,...*) yields double

16. MOD, Modulo. Return the smallest positive remainder that can be subtracted from the first argument to make it exactly divisible by the second argument. e.g., MOD($-29,6$) yields 1 because $-29-1 = -30$, which is exactly divisible by 6. MOD($-29,-6$) yields 1, MOD($29,6$) yields 5, MOD($29,-6$) yields 5.

MOD(*integer,integer*) yields integer   MOD(*expression,expression*)
AMOD(*real,real*) yields real   (not complex)
DMOD(*dbl,dbl*) yields double

17. REAL, Find the real part of a complex number.

REAL(*complex*) yields real   REAL(*complex*)
DREAL(*dbl-complex*) yields double

REAL may also be used as a pseudovariable to assign a real number or the real part of a complex number to the real part of a complex number.

$$REAL(complex) = value;$$

18. ROUND, Round a number. Return the value of the first argument rounded at the digit specified by the second argument. The digit at which to round is numbered as shown.

$$
\begin{array}{ccccccccc}
... & -2 & -1 & 0 & 1 & 2 & 3 & ... \\
... & 9 & 9 & 9 & 9 & 9 & 9 & ... \\
\end{array}
$$

ROUND($-2.376,2$) yields -2.380, ROUND($237.6,0$) yields 238.0, ROUND($237.6,-1$) yields 240.0.

No equivalent function in FORTRAN.   ROUND(*expression,digit*) (For floating-point numbers, *digit* is ignored, and the low-order bit is set to 1.)

19. SIGN, Determine the sign of a number.

The sign of the second argument is transfered to the first argument. For example, ISIGN($5,-3$) yields -5.

    ISIGN(*integer,integer*) yields integer
    SIGN(*real,real*) yields real
    DSIGN(*dbl,dbl*) yields double

Return a FIXED BIN(15) result; -1 if argument is less than zero, 0 if argument is zero, or 1 if argument is greater than zero.

    SIGN(*expression*) yields -1, 0, or 1
    (not complex)

20. SNGL/FLOAT, Convert double-precision number to single-precision floating-point. Truncates argument to single-precision floating-point.

    SNGL(*dbl*) yields real   FLOAT(*dbl*,6) yields FLOAT(6)

The following functions control the precision of arithmetic operations upon two values. The two values may be any arithmetic expression. Each value is first converted to the specified precision, all operations are performed at this precision, and the result is of the specified precision.

21. ADD, Add two values, controlling the precision.

Not in FORTRAN.   The function yields $a + b$ with precision (w,d) for fixed-point or precision (w) for floating-point. Precede a or b with a minus sign to subtract.

ADD(a,b,w,d) fixed-point
ADD(a,b,w) floating-point
ADD(7.8,3.4,2,0) yields 10.0 with precision (2,0).

22. DIVIDE, Divide two values, controlling the precision.

Not in FORTRAN.

The function yields a/b with precision (w,d) for fixed-point or precision (w) for floating-point.

DIVIDE(a,b,w,d) fixed-point
DIVIDE(a,b,w) floating-point

23. MULTIPLY, Multiply two values, controlling the precision.

Not in FORTRAN.

The function yields $a * b$ with precision (w,d) for fixed-point or precision (w) for floating-point.

MULTIPLY(a,b,w,d) fixed-point
MULTIPLY(a,b,w) floating-point

24. PRECISION, Convert a number to a specified precision.

Not in FORTRAN.

The function converts the *expression* to precision (w,d) if fixed-point or precision (w) if floating-point.

PRECISION(*expression*,w,d)
fixed-point
PRECISION(*expression*,w)
floating-point

II. MATHEMATICAL FUNCTIONS

1. ERF, Error function.

ERF(*real*) yields real
DERF(*dbl*) yields double

ERF(*expression*)   (not complex)

2. ERFC, Complement of error function $(1 - \text{ERF})$.

ERFC(*real*) yields real
DERFC(*dbl*) yields double

ERFC(*expression*)   (not complex)

3.   EXP, e^x function.

EXP(*real*) yields real   EXP(*expression*)
DEXP(*dbl*) yields double
CEXP(*complex*) yields complex

4.   LOG, to base e function.

ALOG(*real*) yields real   LOG(*expression*)
DLOG(*dbl*) yields double
CLOG(*complex*) yields complex

5.   LOG2, Log to base 2 function.

No equivalent function in FORTRAN.   LOG2(*expression*)   (not complex)

6.   LOG10, Log to base 10 function.

ALOG10(*real*) yields real   LOG10(*expression*)   (not complex)
DLOG10(*dbl*) yields double

7.   SQRT, Square root function.

SQRT(*real*) yields real   SQRT(*expression*)
DSQRT(*dbl*) yields double
CSQRT(*complex*) yields complex

8.   SIN, Sine function.

SIN(*real-radians*) yields real   SIN(*expression-in-radians*)
DSIN(*dbl-radians*) yields double   SIND(*expression-in-degrees*)
CSIN(*complex-radians*) yields complex   (not complex)

9.   COS, Cosine function.

COS(*real-radians*) yields real   COS(*expression-in-radians*)
DCOS(*dbl-radians*) yields double   COSD(*expression-in-degrees*)
CCOS(*complex-radians*) yields complex   (not complex)

10.   TAN, Tangent function.

TAN(*real-radians*) yields real   TAN(*expression-in-radians*)
DTAN(*dbl-radians*) yields double   TAND(*expression-in-degrees*)
                                                           (not complex)

11.   COTAN, Cotangent function.

COTAN(*real-radians*) yields real   No equivalent function in PL/I.
DCOTAN(*dbl-radians*) yields double

12.   ASIN, Arc sine function.

ASIN(*real*) yields real radians   ASIN(*expression*) yields radians† (not
DARSIN(*dbl*) yields double radians   complex)

13.   ACOS, Arc cosine function.

ACOS(*real*) yields real radians   ACOS(*expression*) yields radians† (not
DARCOS(*dbl*) yields double radians   complex)

† May not be in all PL/I implementations.

14. ATAN, Arc tangent function.

Arc tangent of x, ATAN(x)
    ATAN(*real*) yields real radians
    DATAN(*dbl*) yields double radians

Arc tangent of x/y, ATAN2(x,y)
    ATAN2(*real,real*) yields real radians

    DATAN2(*dbl,dbl*) yields double radians

Arc tangent of x, ATAN(x)
    ATAN(*expression*) yields radians
    ATAND(*expression*) yields degrees (not complex)
Arc tangent of x/y, ATAN(x,y)
    ATAN(*x,y*) yields radians
        (not complex)
    ATAND(*x,y*) yields degrees
        (not complex)

15. SINH, Hyperbolic sine function.

SINH(*real*) yields real
DSINH(*dbl*) yields double

SINH(*expression*)

16. COSH, Hyperbolic cosine function.

COSH(*real*) yields real
DCOSH(*dbl*) yields double

COSH(*expression*)

17. TANH, Hyperbolic tangent function.

TANH(*real*) yields real
DTANH(*dbl*) yields double

TANH(*expression*)

18. ATANH, Inverse hyperbolic tangent function.

No equivalent function in FORTRAN.

ATANH(*expression*)

III. ARRAY FUNCTIONS

1. DIM, Find the extent of a specified dimension of an array.

Not in FORTRAN.

DIM(*array,dimension*)
DIM(A,2) If A is declared as A(5,10:20),
    DIM(A,2) yields 11.

2. HBOUND, Find the upper bound of a specified dimension of an array.

Not in FORTRAN.

HBOUND(*array,dimension*)
If A is declared as A(5,10:20),
HBOUND(A,2) yields 20.

3. LBOUND, Find the lower bound of a specified dimension of an array.

Not in FORTRAN.

LBOUND(*array,dimension*)
If A is declared as A(5,10:20),
LBOUND(A,2) yields 10.

4. POLY, Form a polynomial expression of two arguments.

Not in FORTRAN.   POLY(*array,element-expression*)
                                                  POLY(*array,array*)

5. PROD, Compute the product of an array.

Not in FORTRAN.   PROD(*array*)
                                                  PROD(A) yields A(1)*A(2)*...*A(n)

6. SUM, Sum the elements of an array.

Not in FORTRAN.   SUM(*array*)
                                                  SUM(A) yields A(1)+A(2)+...+A(n)

IV. STRING FUNCTIONS

1. ALL, Logical *and* all bits of a bit-string array.

Not in FORTRAN.   ALL(*bit-string-array*) yields a single bit-string of the same length as the elements of the array. The bits in the result are set to '1'B if all the corresponding bits in the array are '1'B; otherwise they are set to '0'B. For example, if A(1) contains '110'B and A(2) contains '010'B, ALL(A) yields '010'B.

2. ANY, Logical *or* all bits of a bit-string array.

Not in FORTRAN.   ANY(*bit-string-array*) yields a single bit-string of the same length as the elements of the array. The bits in the result are set to '1'B if any corresponding bits in the array are '1'B; otherwise they are set to '0'B. For example, if A(1) contains '110'B and A(2) contains '010'B, ANY(A) yields '110'B.

3. BIT, Convert an expression to a bit-string.

Not in FORTRAN.   The BIT function converts an expression to a bit-string of the specified length according to the rules described in Chapter 6. The *length* must be a decimal integer constant.

BIT(*expression,length*)

4. BOOL, Apply Boolean operations to two bit-strings.

Not in FORTRAN.   BOOL(*string1,string2,operation*) If the two strings are of unequal length, the shorter is extended with zeros. The operation is a bit-string of length 4 that describes the result of each bit-by-bit operation upon the two strings. Four bits are required because there are four possible single-bit combinations of the first and second strings: (0,0), (0,1), (1,0), and (1,1). The *operation* is specified as follows:

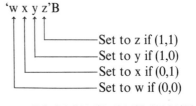

'w x y z'B

Set to z if (1,1)
Set to y if (1,0)
Set to x if (0,1)
Set to w if (0,0)

BOOL('101'B,'001'B,'1001'B) yields
'011'B

5. CHAR, Convert an expression to a character-string of a specified length.

Not in FORTRAN.   The CHAR function converts an expression to a character-string of the specified length according to the rules described in Chapter 6. The *length* must be a decimal integer constant.

CHAR(*expression,length*)

6. HIGH, Create a character-string containing high values.

Not in FORTRAN.   The HIGH function creates a character-string of the specified length containing the highest character in the collating sequence. The *length* must be a decimal integer constant.

HIGH(*length*)

7. INDEX, Find a substring within a character or bit-string.

Not in FORTRAN.

INDEX(*string,substring*) yields the number of the first element of the *string* that matches the *substring*, or zero if there is no match.

8. LENGTH, Find the length of a varying-length character or bit-string.

Not in FORTRAN.

LENGTH(*string*) yields a number containing the length of the *string*, or zero if it is a null string.

9. LOW, Create a character-string containing low values.

Not in FORTRAN.

The LOW function creates a character-string of the specified length containing the highest character in the collating sequence. The *length* must be a decimal integer constant.

LOW(*length*)

10. REPEAT, Repeat a string.

Not in FORTRAN.

The REPEAT function creates a new bit- or character-string by repeating the substring $n+1$ times. The *n* must be a decimal integer constant.

REPEAT(*substring,n*)
REPEAT('AB',2) yields 'ABABAB'.

11. STRING, Concatenate the elements of an array or structure.

Not in FORTRAN.

The STRING function yields a bit- or character-string created by concatenating all of the elements of the array or structure.

(All elements must be bit- or character-strings.)

> STRING(*array*)

STRING may also be used as a pseudo-variable. It assigns the string to each of the elements of the array or structure.

> STRING(*array*) = *string*;

12. SUBSTR, Substring function.

Not in FORTRAN.

SUBSTR(*string,nth,number*) yields a varying-length string containing the *number* of characters (or bits), starting with the nth, from the *string*.

> SUBSTR(*string,nth,number*) =
> > *expression*;
> (The *expression* is converted to a string if it is not already, and *number* characters (or bits) are stored in the nth and succeeding positions of the *string*.)

13. TRANSLATE, Convert occurrences of specified characters or bits within a string to other characters or bits.

Not in FORTRAN.

The TRANSLATE function examines each character or bit in the *source-string* to see if it is in the *mask-string*. If it matches the nth character or bit in the *mask-string*, it is replaced by the nth character or bit in the *replacement-string*.

> TRANSLATE(*source-string,*
> > *replacement-string,mask-string*)
> TRANSLATE('1,225,321.67','9.,','1,.')
> yields '9.225.329,67 as each 1 is replaced by a 9, each comma by a period, and each period by a comma.

14. UNSPEC, Obtain the binary representation of an item.

Not in FORTRAN.

UNSPEC(*expression*) yields a bit-string containing the binary representation of the expression.

UNSPEC(*variable*) = *expression*;
(A bit-string containing the binary representation of the expression is stored in the variable.)

15. VERIFY, Verify the presence of items within a character- or bit-string.

Not in FORTRAN.

VERIFY(*string,pattern-string*) yields zero if all characters (or bits) in the first *string* appear somewhere in the *pattern-string*; otherwise the position of the first character in the *string* not to match is returned.

V. SPECIAL FUNCTIONS

1. ALLOCATION, Determine if storage is allocated for a controlled variable.

Not in FORTRAN.

The ALLOCATION function returns a value of '1'B if storage has been allocated for the *controlled-variable*; otherwise it returns a value of '0'B.

ALLOCATION(*controlled-variable*)

2. COUNT, Count the number of data items transmitted.

Not in FORTRAN.

The COUNT function counts the number of data items transmitted by the last GET or PUT statement for a specified file.

COUNT(*file-name*)

3. DATE, Calendar date of computer run.

A date function is provided in a few compilers, and where it is not provided, many installations have written date functions of their own.

DATE yields '*yymmdd*' as a character-string. *yy*-year, *mm*-month, *dd*-day.

4. LINENO, Find the current line number.

Not in FORTRAN.

The LINENO function returns the number of the current line on the page for a PRINT file.

LINENO(*file-name*)

5. PRIORITY, Determine the relative priority of a task.

Not in FORTRAN.

The PRIORITY function returns the priority relative to the current task of the named task.

PRIORITY(*task-name*)

PRIORITY may also appear on the right-hand side of the assignment statement as a pseudovariable to set the priority of the named task relative to the current task.

PRIORITY(*task-name*) =
relative-priority;

6. TIME, Current clock time on computer.

A time function is provided in a few compilers, and where it is not provided, many installations have written time functions of their own.

TIME yields '*hhmmssttt*' as a character-string. *hh*-hour, *mm*-minute, *ss*-second, *ttt*-thousands of a second.

VI. EXERCISES

1. Use a built-in function to force the computations in the following arithmetic statement to be performed in floating-point.

$$I = J*K/L \qquad\qquad I = J*K/L;$$

2. Replace all of the element values in a floating-point array named VAL with their square roots. VAL has dimensions (10,20).

3. Write a function named KOUNT that examines an integer number and counts the number of occurrences of the integer 1. For example, KOUNT(71241) would equal 2 and KOUNT(-1101) would equal 3. Use the MOD built-in function to extract the digits.

4. Use built-in functions to solve the following equations. (θ is in degrees.)

$$y = \frac{e^x}{\sqrt{z}}\,[\cos(\theta)]$$

$$x = \left|\frac{y}{z}\right|\,[\log_e(w)]$$

5. Extract the first digit to the left of the decimal point of a floating-point variable TOTAL and store it as an integer in I. Extract the first digit to the right of the decimal point, and store it as an integer in J. Both I and J must have the same sign as TOTAL.

6. Use built-in functions to write a function named SWITCH that switches the first and last character of a variable-length character-string. For example, SWITCH('ABYZ') would equal 'ZBYZ', and SWITCH('LMN') would equal 'NML'. (PL/I only).

Chapter 10

Input/Output

FORTRAN input/output is *record* oriented. Each READ or WRITE statement transmits one or more complete logical records (print line, card image, etc.). Records are usually transmitted under the control of a FORMAT statement that directs the conversion of the data between character form and internal computer form. Records may also be transmitted unformatted with no conversion. The variables to be read into or written from are listed in the READ or WRITE statements for both formatted and unformatted I/O. Some FORTRAN compilers also permit data to be read in as a continuous stream of characters in which the data itself names the variables into which the data are to be stored. This form of I/O is termed NAMELIST in FORTRAN, and the data is transmitted in the form on an assignment statement, without regard to any particular columns. For example, the data is of the form A = 3, B = 7.).

PL/I input/output is both *record* and *stream* oriented. *Record* I/O transmits one or more complete logical records at a time, but in PL/I, no format control is possible. *Stream* I/O treats the data as a continuous stream of characters, ignoring the physical record boundaries such as line size or card columns. Stream I/O can be processed in three modes: data directed, list directed, and edit directed. Data-directed I/O is similar to the FORTRAN NAMELIST in which the data is transmitted in the form of an assignment statement (A = 3, B = 7, etc.). List-directed input associates a list of variables one-to-one with a stream of data separated by blanks or commas, and list-directed output prints a list of variables as a stream of values separated by blanks. Edit-directed I/O associates a list of variables with the data under the direction of a FORMAT clause.

The FORTRAN NAMELIST and PL/I data-directed I/O are sometimes useful for quick-and-dirty jobs, but quite useful for debugging. Data directed I/O is slower than formatted I/O. PL/I list-directed I/O has few uses. The formatted I/O is used for printed output, and for reading source data that are in character form. FORTRAN unformatted and PL/I record I/O are faster than the other forms because no conversion is performed. Unformatted I/O is generally used for writing files as contrasted with printing reports.

I. FILE DEFINITION

FORTRAN

FORTRAN data sets or files are numbered 1 to 99. Some older implementations assign file numbers to specific I/O devices, but today the device assignments are usually specified on a job or run control card. There are no universal file numbering conventions, but file 5 is usually the card reader, file 6 the printer, and file 7 the card punch.

PL/I

PL/I data sets or files are assigned a valid PL/I name, termed a *file-name*. File-names are limited to seven characters on S/360/370. The name is associated with a specific I/O device by a Job Control Language card; the file-name is the ddname.

FORTRAN	PL/I
There is no FORTRAN file declaration.	Files are usually defined explicitly in a DCL statement. However, they need not be because PL/I will know a name is a file-name if it is used as a file-name in an I/O statement. The DCL statement is written as:

DCL (*file-name,file-name,...*) FILE;

or

DCL *file-name* FILE;

II. OPENING AND CLOSING FILES

Opening a file allocates buffers to the file, loads access routines into core, checks file labels, and positions the I/O device to the start of the file. If the computer allocates storage dynamically, opening a file can require a sudden increase in the amount of core storage used by the program. Closing a file writes out any remaining records in the output buffers and releases them, writes an end-of-file on output files, rewinds tape reels, and releases any dynamically allocated storage obtained when the file was opened.

FORTRAN	PL/I
Files are opened automatically when the file is first read or written, and closed automatically when the program terminates.	Files are opened automatically when the file is first read or written, and closed automatically when the program terminates.
FORTRAN cannot open files except by reading or writing them. The REWIND statement closes a file and repositions it to its starting point. The general form of the REWIND statement is:	The OPEN and CLOSE statements allow files to be opened and closed under programmer control. Files may be opened explicitly to ensure that there is enough core storage for buffers, and because it is more efficient to open several files with a single OPEN statement. INPUT or OUTPUT may be specified as an attribute in the OPEN statement. Files may be closed explicitly to release core storage, or to allow a file to be read within the same program that wrote it. The general forms of the OPEN and CLOSE statements are:

REWIND *file*

file is the file number, 1 to 99, and can be an integer constant or variable.

REWIND 2
REWIND INDEX

OPEN FILE(*file-name*) INPUT,
    FILE(*file-name*) OUTPUT,...;
CLOSE FILE(*file-name*),
        FILE(*file-name*),...;
OPEN FILE(RET) OUTPUT;
CLOSE FILE(RET);

FORTRAN	PL/I
The END FILE statement writes an end-of-file on a file. It is seldom used because an end-of-file is automatically written when the	An end-of-file is automatically written on PL/I files when the file is closed.

program terminates. The general form is:

> END FILE *file*

The BACKSPACE statement backspaces one logical record. It permits a sequential data set to be 'backed up,' spacing past records already read, enabling them to be reread. The general form is:

> BACKSPACE *file*

No equivalent in PL/I.

III. FORMATTED I/O

Formatted I/O statements transmit data to and from a list of data items under format control. Transmission continues from left to right until all data items have been transmitted.

The READ statement reads data, and the WRITE statement writes data.

	READ (*file,fmt*,END = *label*,
	ERR = *label*) *data-list*
fmt	FORMAT(*format-list*)
	WRITE (*file,fmt*) *data-list*
fmt	FORMAT(*format-list*)

file is an integer constant or variable specifying the file number 1 to 99, *fmt* is the label of a FORMAT statement, and the END and ERR are optional key words that transfer control to a specified statement if an end-of-file is read or a read error occurs. *data-list* names the variables to transmit, and *format-list* specifies the format.

	READ (5,100) I,B
100	FORMAT(I6,F7.2)
	WRITE (6,200) I,J,X
200	FORMAT(I2,I3,F4.1)

The GET statement reads data, and the PUT statement writes data.

> GET FILE(*file-name*) EDIT (*data-list*)
> (*format-list*);
>
> PUT FILE(*file-name*) EDIT (*data-list*)
> (*format-list*);

file-name is the name of the file, *data-list* names the items to transmit, and *format-list* specifies the format.

> GET FILE(F5) EDIT (I,B) (F(6),
> F(7,2));
> PUT FILE(F6) EDIT (I,J,X)
> (F(2),F(3),F(4,1));

PL/I can also specify a remote FORMAT statement similar to the way in which it is done in FORTRAN by coding R(*label*) in place of the format-list. The *label* is the label of a FORMAT statement.

> GET FILE(*file-name*) EDIT (*data-list*)
> (R(*label*));
> *label*: FORMAT(*format-list*);
> GET FILE(F5) EDIT (I,B) (R(S100));
> S100: FORMAT(F(6),F(7,2));

Three special I/O statements are provided by many compilers, including the WATFOR and WATFIV compilers, for the standard I/O units. READ reads card input, PRINT prints on the printer, and PUNCH punches cards.

Two standard files are automatically defined in S/360/370 PL/I; SYSIN for input and SYSPRINT as a PRINT file for output. If GET or PUT statements omit the FILE clause, SYSIN and SYSPRINT are assumed respectively.

READ *fmt,data-list*
 Same as following statement where *file* defines the card reader.

GET EDIT...
 Same as:

READ (*file,fmt*) *data-list*
PRINT *fmt,data-list*
 (Same as following statement where *file* defines the printer.)

GET FILE(SYSIN) EDIT...
PUT EDIT...
 (Same as:)

WRITE (*file,fmt*) *data-list*
PUNCH *fmt,data-list*
 (Same as following statement where *file* defines the card punch.)
WRITE (*file,fmt*) *data-list*

PUT FILE(SYSPRINT) EDIT...

COPY and SKIP options can be included in GET statements, and SKIP, PAGE, and LINE options can be included in PUT statements. COPY writes the input data onto the standard output file SYSPRINT as it is read in by a GET statement. The following statement prints out the values of A and B as they are read in.

GET FILE(F8) COPY EDIT (A,B)
    (F(3),F(6));

SKIP skips a specified number of records on input or output; it takes effect before any data is transmitted.

GET FILE(F8) SKIP(2) EDIT...
PUT FILE(F9) SKIP(N) EDIT...

PAGE starts a new page for a PRINT file; it takes effect before any LINE option and before any variables are transmitted.

PUT FILE(F8) PAGE EDIT...

LINE skips to a specified line on the page; it takes effect before any variables are transmitted.

PUT FILE(F9) LINE(50) EDIT...

SKIP, LINE, and PAGE can also appear without the EDIT clause.

GET FILE(F8) SKIP;
PUT FILE(F9) PAGE, LINE(5);
PUT PAGE;

A. Logical Records

FORTRAN reads and writes logical records. The first item in the format-list automatically starts a new record, and consequently each READ and WRITE statement begins a new logical record.

PL/I considers data in formatted I/O to be a continuous stream of characters irrespective of the logical record boundaries, and each GET and PUT statement continues transmission where the last GET or PUT statement left off. Unfortunately, data seldom exists in real life as a continuous stream of characters, but is organized into logical records such as print lines and card images.

	READ (8,200) A
200	FORMAT(F6.2) (Fields 1 to 6 of the first record are read.)
	READ(8,200) B (Fields 1 to 6 of the second record are read.)

GET FILE(F8) EDIT (A) (R(S200));
S200: FORMAT(F(6,2)); (Fields 1 to 6 of the first record are read.)
GET FILE(F8) EDIT (A) (R(S200));
(Fields 7 to 12 of the first record are read.)

The slash (/) format-item begins a new logical record. Processing the first item in a FORMAT statement has the same effect as a slash, and so n slashes at the beginning of a format-list skip n records; elsewhere n slashes skip $n-1$ records. The slash is processed even if the data-list is exhausted.

SKIP(n) begins a new logical record. n specifies the relative record position; for example, 1 for the next record, 2 for the second record. n can be a constant, variable, or expression, and it is truncated to integer if necessary. SKIP is equivalent to SKIP(1). n may be zero or negative for PRINT files; the effect is a carriage return without line spacing. SKIP is ignored if the data-list is exhausted.

	WRITE (6,100) A,B
100	FORMAT(/,F6.0,/,F6.0,//)

PUT FILE(F6) EDIT (A,B) (R(S100));
S100: FORMAT(SKIP,F(6),SKIP,F(6),
SKIP(2));

The above statements result in the following actions:

- Carriage return caused by start of format-list.
- Carriage return caused by slash, resulting in blank line being printed as line 1.

- No carriage return at start of format-list.
- Carriage return caused by SKIP.

- A is printed on line 2.
- Carriage return caused by slash.
- B is printed on next line 3.
- Two carriage returns caused by slashes, resulting in one blank line being written as line 4.

WRITE (6,100) C

- Carriage return caused by start of format-list.
- Carriage return caused by slash, resulting in blank line being printed as line 5.
- C is printed on next line 6.

- A is printed on line 1.
- Carriage return caused by SKIP.
- B is printed on next line 2.
- SKIP(2) is ignored because the data-list is exhausted.

PUT FILE(F6) EDIT (C)
(R(S100));

- No carriage return at start of next format-list.
- Carriage return caused by SKIP.

- C is printed on next line 3.

The COLUMN format-item, usually abbreviated to COL, permits complete logical records to be easily transmitted with formatted I/O. COL is usually used with PRINT files to skip to a specific column on a page for printing. However, COL may be used with all formatted I/O. COL(n) positions the file to the nth character position in the record, where n is a nonnegative expression that is truncated to integer each time it is encountered in the format-list. (COL is ignored if it is encountered after the data-list is exhausted.) If n is greater than the current file position, fields are skipped on input or blanks are transmitted on output until the nth character position is reached. If n is less than the current file position, the remainder of the current record is ignored on input or padded with blanks on output, and the next record is started at the nth position. No action occurs if n is equal to the current file position. Hence coding COL(1) as the first format-item always positions the file to the start of the next logical record.

GET FILE(PNT) EDIT (A,B)
(COL(1),(2)F(4));
PUT FILE(PNT) EDIT (A,B)
(COL(1),(2)F(4));

B.   Data-list

The data-list can consist of element variables, elements of arrays, and array names; each separated by commas. If an array name

The data-list can consist of element variables, elements of arrays and structures, arrays, structures, and pseudovariables;

is listed, the entire array is read or written, with the leftmost subscript increasing most rapidly. The WATFOR and WATFIV compilers permit expressions in the data-list of WRITE statements.

each separated by commas. The PUT statement can additionally include expressions and literals and constants. If an array name is listed, the entire array is read or written, with the rightmost subscript increasing most rapidly.

WRITE (7,200) A,B(2,3),C

PUT FILE(F7) EDIT (A,B(2,3),C,
'TITLE',100*N/4) (R(S200));

An implied DO-loop can be used within the data-list to transmit all or portions of an array. The same general rules apply to the implied DO-loop as for normal DO-loops as described in Chapter 3. The implied DO-loop is written as:

$(v(i), i = m1,m2,m3)$ or
$(v(i) i = m1,m2)$ $(m3=1$ assumed)

WRITE (3,300) (C(I),I=1,3)

(Same as:)
WRITE (3,300) C(1),C(2),C(3)

$(v(i)$ DO $i = m1$ TO $m2$ BY $m3)$ or
$(v(i)$ DO $i = m1$ TO $m2)$
$(m3=1$ assumed)
PUT FILE(F3) EDIT ((C(I) DO I =
1 TO 3))

(Same as:)
PUT FILE(F3) EDIT (C(1),C(2),C(3))

The WHILE clause can also be used in an implied DO-loop.

(C(I) DO I = 1 TO 100
WHILE(I < N/2))

Implied DO-loops can be nested by enclosing each inner DO-loop in parentheses. The following implied DO-loop transmits A(1,1) to A(1,10), A(2,1) to A(2,10), etc.

((A(I,J),J=1,10),I=1,5)

((A(I,J) DO J=1 TO 10) DO I=1
TO 5)

On input, each item in the data-list is transmitted before processing the next item. Thus an implied DO-loop can use an item read in just prior.

I,(A(J), J=1,I)

(I,(A(J) DO J = 1 TO I))

C. Formats

1. FORMAT statement

The FORMAT statement can be placed anywhere in the program, as it is not executed. Several READ or WRITE statements can use the same FORMAT statement.

The format-list is a part of the GET or PUT statement.

FORTRAN	PL/I

READ (8,100) A,B

100   FORMAT(2F10.2)

GET FILE(F8) EDIT (A,B)
((2)F(10,2));

A remote FORMAT statement can be specified in place of the format-list. It is coded as R(*label*), where *label* is the label of a FORMAT statement, or a label variable that contains the label of the FORMAT statement.

GET FILE(*file-name*) EDIT (*data-list*)
(R(*label*));
label: FORMAT(*format-list*);

The FORMAT statement can be placed anywhere in the program, as it is not executed. Several GET or PUT statements can use the same FORMAT statement.

GET FILE(F8) EDIT (A,B) (R(F100));
F100: FORMAT((2)F(10,2));

2. Variable formats

Formats can be read in as data into an array during execution to allow variable formats. The format to be read in must be of the form:

(*format-list*)

Not in PL/I.

For example, suppose that the following format is contained on a card.

(2I6,F5.2)

The format could be read into array FMT as follows, assuming a computer with four characters per word.

DIMENSION FMT(3)
READ(5,200) (FMT(I),I=1,3)
200   FORMAT(3A4)

The array FMT can now be used in place of a FORMAT statement.

WRITE (10,FMT) I,J,X
(This is equivalent to:)
WRITE (10,300) I,J,X
300   FORMAT(2I6,F5.2)

3. Format-list

Items in the format-list must be separated by commas or slashes.

I6,I1/I2,/,I3//,I9,/,/, etc.

Items in the format-list must be separated by commas.

F(6),F(1),SKIP,F(2),SKIP,F(3),
SKIP(2),F(9),SKIP(2), etc.

A repetition factor can precede an individual format-item, or a group of format-items enclosed in parentheses. The repetition factor must be a positive integer constant.

A repetition factor can precede an individual format-item, or a group of format-items enclosed in parentheses. The repetition factor is an expression enclosed in parentheses, which is truncated to integer if necessary. A zero or negative value causes the format-item to be skipped, and the data-list is associated with the next format-item.

(3I6,2(I3,I4))   Same as:
(I6,I6,I6,I3,I4,I3,I4)

((3)F(6),(2)(F(3),F(4)))   Same as:
(F(6),F(6),F(6),F(3),F(4),F(3),F(4))

((X + Y)F(6),(Z/2.3)(F(3),F(4)))
X + Y and Z/2.3 are evaluated and truncated to integer for use as the repetition factor.

The data-list is associated left-to-right, item-for-item with the format-list.

```
            WRITE (8,100) (J(I),I = 1,3),K
100         FORMAT(I3,I2,2I6)
```
Associated as follows: J(1) with I3, J(2) with I2, J(3) with I6, K with I6.

```
PUT FILE(F8) EDIT ((J(I) DO I = 1
         TO 3),K) (F(3),F(2),(2)F(6));
```
Associated as follows: J(1) with F(3), J(2) with F(2), J(3) with F(6), K with F(6).

Transmission stops when the data-list is exhausted.

```
            WRITE (8,100) A
100         FORMAT(F6.2,A3)
                (Only F6.2 is used.)
```

```
PUT FILE(F8) EDIT (A) (F(6,2),
                       A(3));
           (Only F(6,2) is used.)
```

If all the format-items are used before the data-list is exhausted, a new record is started. The format-list is reused from the left unless it contains a group repeat specification, in which case the rightmost group repeat specification is reused.

If all the format-items are used before the data-list is exhausted, a new record is *not* started (unless a complete record happens to have been transmitted), but the format-list is reused.

```
100         FORMAT(2(I6,I3),3(I8,I4))
```
(Control returns to 3(I8,I4) if the format-list is exhausted.)
```
200         FORMAT(I3,4F6.2)
```
Control returns to I3 if the format-list is exhausted.)

```
((2)(F(6),F(3)),(3)(F(8),F(4)))
```
(Control returns to (2)(F(6),F(3)) if the format-list is exhausted.)
```
(F(3),(4)F(6,2))
```
(Control returns to F(3) if the format-list is exhausted.)

Some format-items, such as the X format-item, are not associated with a data-item, but are processed as they are encountered in the format-list.

FORTRAN	PL/I
FORTRAN items (T, X, H, and literals) are processed even if the data-list is exhausted.	PL/I items (COLUMN, X, LINE, PAGE, and SKIP) are *not* processed if the data-list is exhausted.

4. Numeric format-items

In the following format-items, w represents the field width, including space for a decimal point and a minus sign, and d represents the number of decimal places to the right of the decimal point. For example, the number -62.85 requires w be at least 6 and d at least 2. If the number being transmitted has more than d decimal places, it is rounded to d decimal places. On input, a plus or minus sign may precede the number; plus is assumed if there is no sign. Blanks are treated as zeros. For example, if w is equal to 4, the following numbers are equivalent: 0003, bb+3, bbb3. On output, no sign is printed for positive numbers, and a minus sign is printed for negative numbers. Leading zeros are suppressed. For example, if w is equal to 4, a -3 is printed as bb$-$3, and a plus 3 as bbb3.

FORTRAN	PL/I
In FORTRAN, w and d must be integer constants.	In PL/I, w and d can be constants, variables, or expressions. They are truncated to integer if necessary.
F6.2,I10	F(6,2),F(10) F(N,2),F((N$-$6)/2.5) (If N contains 12, the above is equivalent to:) F(12,2),F(2)

a. Integer format-items. Used to transmit numbers such as 172635, 26 and 8.

FORTRAN	PL/I
Iw I6,I2,I1	F(w) F(6),F(2),F(1)
The number transmitted cannot contain a decimal point.	A decimal point in the number transmitted causes it to be truncated at the decimal point.

b. Single-precision floating-point format-item. Used to transmit numbers such as 264.21, 2.9 and 8.325.

FORTRAN	PL/I
Fw.d F6.2,F3.1,F5.3	F(w,d) F(6,2),F(3,1),F(5,3)

Used to transmit numbers such as $-347.26E-17$ or 0.25629E2.

FORTRAN	PL/I
Ew.d E11.2,E9.5	E(w,d) E(11,2),E(9,5)

Can also be coded as E(w,d,s) for output, where s is the number of significant digits to print. When s is omitted, it is assumed to be $d + 1$. The number 116.231 is printed as b1.1623E$+$02 for E(11,4), and b1162.3E$-$01 for E(11,1,5).

c. Double-precision floating-point format-item. Used to transmit numbers such as 347.264E17.

D$w.d$ D11.2,D9.5   No special format, use E(w,d) or F(w,d).

d. Generalized format-item. Used for any type of number.

G$w.d$ G8.2,G12.6   No special PL/I generalized format-item.
G format acts as I, F, or E; depending on   All PL/I formats are generalized and can be
the form of the data. On output, E or F for-   used with any numeric data. PL/I cannot
mat is selected based on the size of the   select the E or F format on output based on
number.   the size of the number.

e. Picture format-item. Used to print numbers such as \$100.20, 1,425.2 or 00032.

Not in FORTRAN.   P'*picture-specification*'   P'999V.99'

                                            Similar to COBOL PICTURE item. It can
                                            suppress or print leading zeros, insert a
                                            comma, dollar sign, credit symbols, etc. See
                                            Chapter 12 for a description of the Picture
                                            format-item.

f. Complex number format-item

Two successive F, E, D, or G format-items   C(*one or two F, E, or P format-items*)
are required for each complex data-item.   If the second format-item is omitted, it is
                                            assumed to be the same as the first. The 'I'
                                            coded in complex constants is not permitted
                                            on input nor printed on output.

F6.1,F6.1   or   2F6.1   C(F(6,1),F(6,1))   or   C(F(6,1))

g. Scale factor. Used to shift the decimal point left or right during transmission.

The scale factor is written as sP, and is   The scale factor is permitted only in F
appended to the left of a D, E, F, or G format- format-items, and is written as F(w,d,s). Like
item (and any repetition factor). The s is an the w and d, s can be a constant, variable, or
integer constant, plus or minus, and it causes expression, plus or minus, and it is truncated
the following scaling to be performed.   to integer if necessary. It causes the following
                                            scaling to be performed.

external number =   *target number =*
              internal number $\times 10^s$ *source number* $\times 10^s$

On input, $+s$ shifts the decimal point s places to the left, and $-s$ shifts it s places to the right. On output, $+s$ shifts it to the right, and $-s$ to the left. For example, 2PF6.1 would cause the number 250.0 to be read as 2.5 on input, and the number 250.0 to be written as 25000.0 on output

On input or output, $+s$ shifts the decimal point s places to the right, and $-s$ shifts it s places to the left. For example, F(6,1,2) would cause the number 250.0 to be read as 25000.0 on input, and the number 250.0 to be written as 25000.0 on output.

The scale factor stays in effect within a FORMAT statement for all following numeric format-items until another scale factor is encountered. A scale factor of 0P will stop scaling.

The scale factor is effective only for the format-item within which it is coded.

5. Character format-items

a. Character format-item

Aw   A4,A2

A(w)   A(4),A(2)

On input, the variable is padded on the right with blanks if the data-item is greater than w. The rightmost characters are stored if the data-item is less than w. (The data-item will contain four, six, or eight characters, depending on the word size of the computer.) On output, the field is padded on the left with blanks if the data-item is smaller than w. The leftmost characters are transmitted if the data-item is larger than w.

On input, the variable is padded on the right with blanks if the data-item is greater than w. The leftmost characters are stored if the data-item is less than w. On output, the field is padded on the right with blanks if the data-item is smaller than w. The leftmost characters are transmitted if the data-item is larger than w.

b. Literal character-string

wHcharacters or 'characters'
6HSOFTER   'SOFTER'

Not permitted in PL/I format-item. Literal character-strings can be used as data-items, but not as format-items.

The literal characters are not associated with a data-item, but are transmitted in the order in which they appear in the format-list. Literal character-strings are normally used for output. On input, w characters are read in, replacing the literal constant. The literal character format-item is processed even if the data-list is exhausted.

WRITE (6,100)

PUT FILE(F6) EDIT ('THIS OUT')
(A(8)):

100   FORMAT(8HTHIS OUT)

6.   Control format-items

a.   Spacing format-item. The spacing format-item skips *w* fields on input, and inserts *w* blanks on output.

Xw   X6,X10

The X format-item is processed even if the data-list is exhausted.

X(w)   X(6),X(10)

The X format-item is not processed if the data-list is exhausted.

b.   Column format-item. The column format-item is normally used for printing lines of output. It skips to a specified column position before transmission. It can be used for both reading and writing.

Tc   T6,T75

On input, reading begins from the *c*th column. On output, writing begins in the *c*th or $c+1$th column, depending on the compiler. T format-items are processed even if the data-list is exhausted. The T format-item remains on the same line if it skips to the left of the current column position.

COL(c)   COL(6),COL(75)

On input, reading begins from the *c*th column, and on output, writing begins in the *c*th column. COL format-items are not processed if the data-list is exhausted. COL starts a new line if it skips to the left of the current column position.

7.   Other format-items

a.   Logical format-item

Lw   L1

T for .TRUE. or F for .FALSE. is read or written.

Not in PL/I.

b.   Bit-string format-item

Not in FORTRAN.

B(w)   B(10),B(2)

The bit-string format-item is the same as the character-string format-item A(w), except that a bit-string containing only ones and zeros is transmitted.

c.   Hexadecimal or Octal format-items

Zw   or   Ow

Hexadecimal or octal data is transmitted, depending on the byte size of the computer. These formats are used almost exclusively on output for debugging.

Not in PL/I.

8. Print control format-items

a. New page

A new page is started by printing the character '1' as the first character of the line.

The PAGE option skips to the first line of
the next page. PAGE can be used only with
PRINT files, and it is ignored if the data-list
is exhausted. PAGE can be coded as a
format-item, or preceding the EDIT.

WRITE (6,100) A

100   FORMAT(1H1,F6.0)

PUT FILE(F6) EDIT (A)
(PAGE,F(6));
or
PUT FILE(F6) PAGE EDIT (A)
(F(6));

b. Skip to a specific line on the page

Not in FORTRAN.

LINE(*line-number*)

LINE spaces down the page to the *line-
number* (1 to 66 on most printers) specified.
If *line-number* is less than the current line,
the ENDPAGE condition is raised, and
unless otherwise programmed, will begin on
line-number of the next page. The *line-number*
can be a constant, variable, or expression,
and it is truncated to integer if necessary.
LINE can be used only with PRINT files,
and it is ignored if the data-list is exhausted.
The following example causes A to be
printed on the 56th line of the page.

PUT FILE(F6) EDIT (A) (LINE(56,
F(6));
or
PUT FILE(F6) LINE(56) EDIT (A)
(F(6));

D. Print Files

FORTRAN print files differ from other files only in that the first character of each record is
not printed, but instead controls the line spacing. Hence for a 132 position print line, up to
133 characters can be written, with the first character controlling the line spacing. Each
print line corresponds to a logical record. PL/I also permits files to be written the same as
FORTRAN, with the first character of each line controlling the line spacing. However, PL/I
files can be declared as PRINT files, permitting the line spacing to be controlled by the SKIP,
PAGE, and LINE options rather than by the first character of the print line. The print control facilities are as follows:

1. Printer control

The first character controls the printer.

The first character can control the printer as in FORTRAN, but if files are declared to be PRINT files, format-items control the printer.

b (blank) Single space before printing.
0 (zero) Double space before printing.
1 (one) Skip to the first line of next
                                page.
+ (plus) Carriage return without line
                                spacing.

SKIP   Single space before printing.
SKIP(2) Double space before printing.
PAGE   Skip to the first line of next
                               page.
SKIP(0) Carriage return without line
                              spacing.

```
        WRITE (6,100) I,J
100     FORMAT(1H1,2I6)
        WRITE (6,110)  ρ
110     FORMAT(1H ,9HNEXT
                        LINE)
```

```
PUT FILE(F6) EDIT (I,J) (PAGE,
                    (2)F(6));
PUT FILE(F6) EDIT ('NEXT LINE')
                    (SKIP,A(9));
```

2. Line-size and page-size

Not in FORTRAN.

The OPEN statement establishes a file as a PRINT file, and can set a line-size and a page-size. The line-size defaults to 120 characters per line and the page-size to 60 lines per page on S/360/370. Most printers have 132 print positions per line, and 66 lines per page. The line-size and page-size are set as follows:

```
OPEN FILE(file-name) PRINT
                LINESIZE(line-size)
                PAGESIZE(page-size);
OPEN FILE(F6) PRINT
        LINESIZE(132) PAGESIZE(66);
```

Printing a line beyond the page-size causes an eject to a new page, unless the ON END-PAGE statement described in Chapter 11 is used. In the following example, the printer skips to line 60, prints a footing, ejects to a new page, and prints a new page number each time the page-size is exceeded. The example also shows how the ON END-PAGE statement, described in Chapter 11, can be used to print page headings.

```
ON ENDPAGE(PNT) BEGIN;
PUT FILE(PNT) EDIT
    ('CONTINUED') (LINE(60),A(9));
```

(Skip to line 60 and print
CONTINUED.)
NPAGE = NPAGE + 1;
(Count a page.)
PUT FILE(PNT) EDIT ('PAGE',
NPAGE) (PAGE,X(100),A(4),F(4));
(Eject to a new page and print the
page number.)
PUT FILE(PNT) SKIP;
(Skip so that the next PUT starts
on a new line.)
END;

A program might be written as follows:

NPAGE = 0;
(Set the page number to zero.)
OPEN FILE(PNT) PRINT
LINESIZE(132) PAGESIZE(54);
(Set the line-size and the page-size.)
SIGNAL ENDPAGE(PNT);
(Print the first page heading.)

Hereafter whenever an attempt is made to write the 54th line, a footing is printed, and a new page is started with the page number printed at the top of the page.

IV. UNFORMATTED I/O

The READ and WRITE statements for unformatted I/O transmit data to and from core without any conversion. Unformatted I/O is more efficient than formatted I/O, and is generally used for writing files to be read by another program, as contrasted with printed reports produced by formatted I/O. Each READ and WRITE statement transmits a single logical record in both FORTRAN and PL/I.

The READ and WRITE statements are identical to the formatted READ and WRITE statements, except that no FORMAT statement is specified.

READ (*file*,END = *label*,
ERR = *label*) *data-list*
WRITE (*file*) *data-list*

The data-list is identical to that of the formatted I/O statements.

The general forms of the READ and WRITE statements that read and write unformatted I/O are as follows:

READ FILE(*file-name*)INTO
(*variable*);
WRITE FILE(*file-name*)FROM
(*variable*);

The *variable* is usually an array, structure, or character-string variable, and its length should equal the logical record length. (The

RECORD condition described in Chapter 11 allows records to be transmitted that are unequal to the record length.) The *variable* cannot be subscripted, or be a subroutine parameter. Records of unknown length are processed by the READ statement setting varying-length character-string variables to the length of the record, and the WRITE statement writing a record whose length is the current length of a varying-length character-string.

READ (9,END = 100) A,B,C	READ FILE(F9) INTO (A);
WRITE (9) A,B,C	WRITE FILE(F9) FROM (A);

Unformatted I/O is termed record I/O in PL/I. The RECORD attribute must be specified in the DCL or OPEN statement if a record I/O file is to be opened explicitly by the OPEN statement.

DCL (*file-name*) FILE RECORD;
or
OPEN FILE(*file-name*) INPUT
RECORD;

Input records are skipped by omitting the data-list in the READ statement.

Input records are skipped by the IGNORE (*number*) clause in the READ statement.

READ (5)

READ FILE(F5) IGNORE(1);

PL/I has additional I/O statements to process indexed-sequential files and teleprocessing data, beyond the scope of this book.

V.   NAMELIST (DATA-DIRECTED) I/O

FORTRAN NAMELIST and PL/I data-directed I/O permit data to be read and written in the form of assignment statements such as A = 3 or B = 7. No format is required, and this type of I/O is especially useful for debugging and quick-and-dirty jobs.

Data to be read or written as NAMELIST data must be declared by the NAMELIST statement. (The WATFOR compiler I/O differs from the normal FORTRAN NAMELIST I/O described here.) The NAMELIST statement must precede any executable statement in the program or subroutine. It is written as follows:

Data-directed files can be declared by the DCL statement and opened and closed by the OPEN and CLOSE statements, as with all PL/I files, but they need not, and seldom are explicitly declared or opened and closed.

NAMELIST /*name-list*/
data-list

DCL (*file-name*) FILE;

The *name-list* is a unique 1 to 6 character name. The *data-list* specifies the variables and arrays that are to be read or written. The following statement declares TA to be a *name-list* associated with the variables I, J, and K; and X10 to be a *name-list* associated with L and M.

$$\text{NAMELIST /TA/I,J,K}$$
$$\text{/X10/L,M}$$

Data is read by the READ statement as follows:

$$\text{READ } (file,name\text{-}list)$$

Input data is in the form of assignment statements separated by commas. Only constants can be used as values, and only variables listed in the NAMELIST statement for the *name-list* can be included, but they may be in any order. Arrays can be subscripted with integer constants. Character data cannot be read in. The data must begin with &*name-list*, preceded and followed by at least one blank, and end with &END. (Some compilers require a dollar sign rather than the ampersand.)

In the example that follows, the data is contained in file 5.

$$\text{b&TAb I}=6, \text{J}=7, \text{K}=6 \text{ &END}$$
$$\text{b&X10bL}=2,$$
$$\text{M}=14 \text{ &END}$$

The data is read in as follows:

$$\text{READ (5,TA)}$$
$$(\text{I}=6, \text{J}=7, \text{ and K}=6 \text{ are}$$
$$\text{read in.})$$
$$\text{READ (5,X10)}$$
$$(\text{L}=2 \text{ and M}=14 \text{ are}$$
$$\text{read in.})$$

Data is written by the WRITE statement.

$$\text{WRITE } (file,name\text{-}list)$$

Data is read by the GET statement as follows:

$$\text{GET FILE}(file\text{-}name) \text{ DATA};$$
$$\text{or}$$
$$\text{GET DATA; (SYSIN file is assumed.)}$$

Input data is in the form of assignment statements separated by commas or blanks. Only constants can be used as values. Arrays may be subscripted. The list of assignment statements is terminated by a semicolon.

In the example that follows, the data is contained in the standard input file SYSIN.

$$\text{I}=6, \text{J}=7, \text{K}=6; \text{L}=2$$

$$\text{M}=14;$$

The data is read in as follows:

$$\text{GET DATA};$$
$$(\text{I}=6, \text{J}=7, \text{ and K}=6 \text{ are read in.})$$

$$\text{GET DATA};$$
$$(\text{L}=2 \text{ and M}=14 \text{ are read in.})$$

Data is written by the PUT statement.

$$\text{PUT FILE}(file\text{-}name) \text{ DATA}$$
$$(data\text{-}list);$$
$$\text{PUT DATA } (data\text{-}list); \text{ (SYSPRINT}$$
$$\text{is assumed.)}$$

All variables associated with the *name-list* in the NAMELIST statement are written in the same format as the input.

All of the items listed in the *data-list* are written in the same format as the input. The *data-list* can contain variables, arrays, or structures. It cannot contain functions, literals, constants, subroutine parameters, based-variables, or DEFINED data items. Arrays may be subscripted. If the data-list is omitted and only PUT DATA; is coded, all variables known within the program are printed. Use this form with discretion.

The PAGE, LINE, and SKIP options may also be used in the PUT DATA statement to control the printer.

> PUT SKIP DATA(A,B,C);
> PUT PAGE LINE(10) DATA(X,Z);

NAMELIST files may only be read and written as name-list files.

DATA may be intermixed with LIST and EDIT to read or write data on the same file.

> PUT PAGE EDIT (X) (A(4));
> PUT SKIP DATA(B);
> PUT SKIP LIST('THE END');

VI. LIST-DIRECTED I/O

Not in FORTRAN.

List-directed I/O is identical to data-directed I/O, except that on input the data consists of a stream of constants separated by blanks or commas, and the GET statement names the variables into which the data is to be read. On output the data is printed as a string of values separated by blanks. The PUT LIST data-list may contain functions, literals, and constants. There are few uses of list-directed I/O. In the following example, the standard input file SYSIN contains the data:

> 2, 3.5, 6, 8;

The GET statement reads the data.

> GET LIST(A,B,C);
>   (A is set to 2, B to 3.5, and C to 6.)
> GET LIST(D);
>   (D is set to 8.)

The PUT statement writes the data.

> PUT LIST(A,B,C,D);
>   (The values of A, B, C, and D are

printed on the standard output file SYSPRINT in the same form in which they appear on input.)

LIST may be intermixed with DATA and EDIT to read or write data on the same file.

VII.   END-OF-FILE AND TRANSMISSION ERRORS

A.   End-of-File

The END=*label* keywork is available on most compilers to transfer to a specified statement when an attempt is made to read past the end-of-file.

The ON ENDFILE(*file-name*) statement described in Chapter 11 specifies the action to take when an attempt is made to read past the end-of-file.

READ (9,100,END=200)
A,B

ON ENDFILE(F9) GO TO S200;
GET FILE(F9) EDIT (A,B) ((2)F(6));

B.   Transmission Errors

The ERR=*label* keywork is available on most compilers to transfer to a specified statement when a read error occurs.

The ON TRANSMIT(*file-name*) statement described in Chapter 11 specifies the action to take when a read or write error occurs.

READ (9,100,ERR=400)
A,B

ON TRANSMIT(F9) GO TO S400;
GET FILE(F9) EDIT (A,B) ((2)F(6));

Both END and ERR can appear in the same READ statement in any order following the file number and format label.

Both ENDFILE and TRANSMIT can be active at the same time.

READ (9,100,END=200,
ERR=400) A,B

ON ENDFILE(F9) GO TO S200;
ON TRANSMIT(F9) GO TO S400;
GET FILE(F9) EDIT (A,B) ((2)F(6));

VIII.   DIRECT-ACCESS FILES

Some FORTRAN and most PL/I compilers support direct-access files. A direct-access file contains records that are identified by a unique key. The key is a sequential number and is not a part of the record. The READ or WRITE statement is given the record key to read or write a specific record. Direct-access can be visualized as an array of records stored on a direct-access storage device in which the array index is the record key. Unlike normal sequential files in which records are processed in the order in which they are stored, direct-access allows specific records to be read or written. A sequential file is analogous to a deck of cards in which one card at a time is dealt from the top to locate the card desired. With direct-access, one could see into the card deck and pluck out the card directly. Direct-access files can reside only on direct-access devices such as disk or drum.

PL/I supports three types of direct-access files, in addition to indexed-sequential files.

(Indexed-sequential files are a combination of direct-access and sequential.) Only the PL/I REGIONAL(1) direct-access files have a counterpart in FORTRAN and are discussed here; the other access methods are beyond the scope of this book.

The record keys must be in ascending numerical order. This enables direct-access files to be processed in a sequential order by incrementing the key with each read or write. PL/I also allows REGIONAL(1) files to be processed sequentially without using the keys. This is faster than accessing them directly with the keys.

PL/I preempts the first byte of each record for a delete flag. When the file is opened for output, PL/I writes the entire file with empty records and sets the delete byte to '11111111'B to indicate that the records are empty. The delete byte does not stop records from being read or written, and one must test the delete byte to determine if a record is deleted.

The DEFINE FILE statement must declare each direct-access file, and it must appear once before any other statements that use the file.	The DCL statement must declare each REGIONAL file as follows.

DEFINE FILE *file*(*max*,
                                    size,*f*,*key*)

file—integer constant that specifies the data set reference number.
max—maximum number of records in the file.

size—maximum size of the records in units specified by *f*.

f—coded as L, E, or U as follows.

    L—*size* in bytes. The file may be processed by formatted or unformatted I/O.

    E—*size* in characters. The file may be processed by formatted I/O only. In S/360/370, the character and byte are both eight bits long. Hence L does all that does E, and more.

    U—*size* in words (four bytes per word) in S/360/370). The file may be processed with unformatted I/O only.

key—integer variable that specifies which record to read or write. Upon completion of the READ or WRITE, *key* is set to the key of the next record in the file. The FIND statement sets *key* to the found record. Records are numbered from 1 to *size*.

DCL FILE(*file-name*) RECORD
    KEYED ENV(REGIONAL(1))
              F(*size*));

file-name—name of the file.

The maximum number of records in the file is specified in the Job Control Language.

size—integer expression giving the record size in bytes. Be sure to allow one byte extra for the delete byte. Records are unblocked, fixed-length.

The key must be a character-string of length 8 containing numeric characters. A variable defined to be PIC '(8)9' is the most convenient for this. Records are numbered from 0 to *max* − 1.

In the following example, file 8 is defined to contain 100 records, each 80 bytes in length.

In the following example, file F8 is defined to contain records 81 bytes long. (One extra byte is required for the delete byte.)

DEFINE FILE 8(100,80,L,
K8)

DCL FILE(F8) RECORD KEYED
ENV(REGIONAL(1) F(81));
DCL K8 PIC '(8)9';

FORTRAN direct-access files must be formatted before being used. The files are automatically formatted when the file is opened by the execution of the first WRITE statement for that file, in combination with the Job Control Language statement specifying that the data set is new; DISP = (NEW,...) in S/360/370.

REGIONAL files must be formatted before being used. This is accomplished by opening the file for output and closing it again. The entire file is written with records containing the delete byte set to the value of '11111111'B. Do not open the file for output again as it will be rewritten with empty records, destroying whatever else is in the file.

OPEN FILE(F8) DIRECT OUTPUT;
CLOSE FILE(F8);

The WRITE statement writes records directly into a direct-access file.

REGIONAL files must first be opened for UPDATE to enable the WRITE statement to write records directly into the file.

OPEN FILE(F8) DIRECT UPDATE;
WRITE FILE(*file-name*) FROM
(*data-list*) KEYFROM(*key*);

WRITE (*file'key, fmt*)
data-list

key—integer expression that specifies the record to write (1 is the first record). *key* is set to the key of the next record in the file upon completion of the WRITE.

key—character-string expression of length 8 that gives the relative record to write (0 is the first record).

fmt—label of format statement for formatted I/O. Omit *fmt* for unformatted I/O.

The following statements write the first and 15th records in file 8.

The following statements write the first and 15th records in file F8.

WRITE (8'1,100) A

K8 = 15
WRITE (8'K8,100) A

WRITE FILE(F8) FROM(A)
KEYFROM(1);
K8 = 15;
WRITE FILE(F8) FROM(A)
KEYFROM(K8);

The READ statement reads records directly from a direct-access file. The *fmt* is omitted for unformatted I/O, and the ERR = *label* is optional.

As with the WRITE statement, REGIONAL files must first be opened for UPDATE for the READ statement to read records directly from the file.

READ (*file'key, fmt,*
ERR = *label*) *data-list*

READ FILE(*file-name*) FROM
(*data-list*) KEYFROM(*key*);

The following statements read the second and third records from file 8. Note that K8 is automatically incremented after the first READ.

```
        K8 = 2
        READ (8′K8,100) A

        READ (8′K8,100) A
```

Direct-access files can be processed in a sequential order by incrementing the key for each successive READ or WRITE. Remember that the key is automatically set to the key of the next record after each READ or WRITE.

```
        DEFINE FILE 8(1000,100,
                            L,KEY)
        KEY = 1

        DO 100 I = 1, 1000
100     READ (8′KEY) A
```

The FIND statement can be used to locate the next record while the current record is being processed. This increases the processing efficiency by overlapping the I/O with the computations. The FIND statement sets the *key* to the found record. The FIND statement is written as follows.

FIND (*file′record*)

record—an integer expression that specifies the key of the record to find.

The loop above could be processed more efficiently by the following use of the FIND statement.

```
        DEFINE FILE 8(1000,100,
                            L,KEY)
        KEY = 1
100     READ (8′KEY) A
        FIND (8′KEY)
        ─
        IF (KEY.LE.1000) GO TO
                            100
```

The following statements read the second and third records from file F8.

```
        K8 = 2;
        READ FILE(F8) FROM (A)
                            KEYFROM(K8);
        READ FILE(F8) FROM (A)
                            KEYFROM(K8 + 1);
```

REGIONAL files can be opened as SE-QUENTIAL INPUT or OUTPUT, permitting them to be processed as normal sequential files. This is more efficient than reading each successive record directly.

```
        DCL FILE(F8) RECORD KEYED
                ENV(REGIONAL(1) F(101));
        OPEN FILE(F8) SEQUENTIAL
                            INPUT;
        ON ENDFILE(F8) GO TO DONE;
NEXT: READ FILE(F8) INTO (A);
        GO TO NEXT;
DONE:
```

IX.   EXERCISES

1.   Write all of the statements to explicitly declare a file, open it for output, write a record into it, close the file, open it again for input, read in all the records it contains, and detect the end-of-file.

2.   An input file consists of 80-column cards divided into six fields, each alternating seven and nine characters long. The last 32 columns of the cards are blank. The first two fields are integer format, the next two fields are floating-point, and the final two fields contain character data. Write a program to read in this file and store each column in an array. Assume that there can be up to 100 records in the file. Print an error message and terminate the job if the end-of-file is not reached by the time the 100th record is read. Print the number of records read in.

3.   Assume that the variables TOTAL, SIZE, FORM, and DIST are to be printed out for debugging purposes, and due to unfamiliarity with the program, it is not known in what format the items are. Write the output statements necessary to print the items.

4.   A variable named LIST contains four characters. Print a line with the first character in column 10, the second character in column 20, the third in column 30, and the fourth in column 40. Use the T or COLUMN format-item to write blank characters to mask out all but the character desired.

5.   Read in a deck of cards containing eight integer numbers per card, 10 columns per number. Store the numbers in a two-dimensional array with the card number as one dimension and the number within the card as the other. Allow for up to 100 cards, and stop reading cards if this number is exceeded. Detect the end-of-file, and write out the array with unformatted I/O. Then read the entire array back into an identical array, and validate that the array was transmitted properly by comparing each element of the first array with the second array.

6.   Print a table containing the square roots of the integers from 1 to 1000. The square roots are to be printed with five significant digits of accuracy to the right of the decimal point. Print 50 lines per page with each line containing two columns of values as shown. Print the page heading at the top of each new page.

	TABLE OF SQUARE ROOTS		PAGE xxx
NUMBER	SQUARE ROOT	NUMBER	SQUARE ROOT
1	1.00000	51	7.14143
2	1.41421	52	7.21110
⋮	⋮	⋮	⋮
50	7.07107	100	10.00000

7.   Write a program to read in a card containing an initial investment, an interest rate, a number of years, and a starting date. The card has the following format:

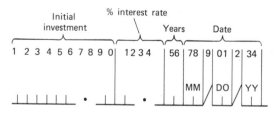

Given this information, you are to produce the following report:

| INVESTMENT ANALYSIS | | | PAGE xxx | |

PREPARED ESPECIALLY FOR: your name
INITIAL INVESTMENT: $xxxxxxx.xx   INTEREST: xx.x%   YEARS: xx

DATE	CURRENT BALANCE	INTEREST EARNED	NEW BALANCE	YEAR
xx/xx/xx	$xxxxxxx.xx	$xxxxxx.xx	$xxxxxxx.xx	xx

Allow 30 lines per page. The interest earned is computed as current balance times interest divided by 100. The new balance is current balance plus interest earned.

8. A card deck consisting of 31 cards must be read that is set up as follows. Column 1 of the first card describes the format of the data contained in the cards that follow. If column 1 contains a 1, the cards following contain an integer number in columns 1 to 5. If column 1 contains a 2, the cards following contain a decimal number with two digits to the right of the decimal point in column 1 to 10. If column 1 contains a 3, the cards following contain an integer number in columns 1 to 4. Read in the file and print out each card as it is read. Store the numbers in a floating-point array named FLOAT. In FORTRAN use variable formats, and in PL/I use a remote format item with label variables.

9. Copy a file containing 380 character records and an unknown number of records. Exclude all records that contain the character 'I' in the 63rd byte position of the record. Print out the number of records read, number excluded, and the number of records written.

Chapter 11

Debugging Aids

Both FORTRAN and PL/I provide compiler diagnostics, the comprehensiveness and clarity of which depend on the particular compiler implementation. PL/I has extensive execution debugging aids; FORTRAN has few. Perhaps the most powerful PL/I debugging aid in the S/360/370 implementation is the facility to print the statement number corresponding to the source listing of a statement causing an error during execution. This feature relies entirely on the compiler implementation, and FORTRAN compilers could, but seldom do, provide this.

I. OPERATOR COMMUNICATIONS

Most installations will control any program communications with the computer operators, both to ensure that the communications are understood and to keep unnecessary communications from distracting the operators.

FORTRAN

The PAUSE statement suspends program execution until the computer operator intervenes. PAUSE is a carryover from the time when programmers operated the computer themselves, and PAUSE would allow the programmer to stop his program and debug it from the console. PAUSE is seldom used today. It is written as follows, where n is any integer.

> PAUSE n

FORTRAN displays the integer n on the operator's console.

> PAUSE 20

PL/I

The DISPLAY statement displays a message to the computer operator, and may also suspend program execution until the operator responds to the message. DISPLAY is written as follows.

> DISPLAY(*expression*);

The *expression* is converted to a character-string if necessary, and is displayed on the operator's console.

> DISPLAY('END OF JOB');

The DISPLAY statement can also request an operator response from the console keyboard. In the following example, the message is displayed to the operator, and program execution is suspended until the operator responds with a message typed in on the console keyboard. This message is stored in ANS.

> DCL ANS CHAR(80);
> DISPLAY('WHAT DAY IS IT?')
>   REPLY(ANS);

II. FORTRAN ERROR CONDITIONS

FORTRAN provides few tests for error conditions, and the following error conditions are not provided by all compilers.

A. Underflow and Overflow

Underflow occurs in multiplication or division of real numbers when the resultant exponent is smaller than the computer can contain. Overflow occurs when the resultant exponent from any arithmetic operation on real numbers is larger than the computer can contain. Underflow and overflow are tested by the following subroutine call.

> CALL OVERFLOW(I)

The overflow condition is turned off, and I represents an integer variable that is set as follows:

> I = 1, exponent overflow
> 2, no overflow or underflow
> 3, exponent underflow

B. Zero Divide Check

The zero divide check occurs when an attempt is made to divide by zero, and is tested by the following subroutine call.

> CALL DVCHK(I)

The divide check is turned off, and I represents an integer variable that is set as follows.

> I = 1, divide check was on
> 2, divide check was off

C. End-of-File

The end-of-file condition can be tested in some compilers by including the 'END=*label*' keyword in the READ statement. In the following example, the READ statement transfers to statement 400 if an attempt is made to read past the end-of-file.

> READ (8,100,END=400) A,B,C

D. Input Transmission Errors

Transmission errors that occur while reading data can be tested in some compilers by including the 'ERR=*label*' keyword in the READ statement. In the following example, the READ statement transfers to statement 1000 if an input transmission error occurs.

> READ (8,100,ERR=1000) A,B,C

Both END and ERR can appear in the same READ statement. They may appear in any order following the file number and format label.

$$READ\ (8,100,END=400,ERR=1000)\ A,B,C$$

III. PL/I ERROR AND CHECKOUT CONDITIONS

PL/I is able to detect error conditions such as zero divide and fixed overflow, as well as several special conditions such as end-of-file and end-of-page. Each of these conditions is associated with a descriptive name, and most can be enabled or disabled by a condition-prefix append to a procedure, or a begin block, or a single statement. Disabled conditions are not detected by PL/I. Enabled conditions are detected and PL/I performs a standard action, usually printing an error message and terminating the job. The ON statement substitutes programmer-supplied statements for the standard action, and allows execution to continue.

The CONVERSION, FIXEDOVERFLOW, OVERFLOW, UNDERFLOW, and ZERODIVIDE conditions are normally enabled, but can be disabled. The CHECK, SIZE, SUBSCRIPTRANGE, STRINGSIZE, and STRINGRANGE conditions are normally disabled, but can be enabled. The CONDITION, ENDFILE, ENDPAGE, ERROR, FINISH, NAME, UNDEFINEDFILE, RECORD, and TRANSMIT conditions are always enabled and cannot be disabled. The conditions are described in detail later in this section.

A. Condition-Prefix

Except for the conditions that are always enabled, conditions are enabled or disabled by appending a *condition-prefix* to the procedure, begin block, or statement within which the conditions are to be enabled or disabled. The general form of the condition-prefix is:

(*condition,condition,...*): *label*: *statement*;

Conditions are enabled by specifying the *condition* names (CHECK, SIZE, etc.) and are disabled by preceding the condition name with NO (NOCHECK, NOSIZE, etc.). The following example enables SIZE and disables ZERODIVIDE within a procedure, and disables SIZE for one statement within the procedure. The condition-prefix applies to all statements within a procedure or begin block, but not to any subroutines or functions that they may invoke.

```
(SIZE,NOZERODIVIDE): COMP: PROC;
                     A = B;
                     (NOSIZE): C = D − E;
                     END COMP;
```

B. ON Statement

The ON statement substitutes programmer-supplied statements for the standard action for selected conditions, and execution is allowed to continue from the point where the condition was raised. The ON statement is an executable statement that becomes effective only after it is executed. (If there are several ON statements for a condition within a block, the last one executed applies.) The ON statement has the same scope as that of names, as described in Chapter 7. An ON statement executed in an inner block or procedure is not effective in an outer block or procedure. The general form of the ON statement is:

ON *condition on-unit*;

The *condition* is any of the condition names. The *on-unit* consists of the statement or statements to be executed when the condition occurs. The on-unit can be either an unlabeled, simple statement (any statement except RETURN, DCL, FORMAT, PROC, IF, ON, or DO) or an unlabeled BEGIN block which may contain any statement except RETURN. After the on-unit is executed, control returns to the point where the condition occurred, unless the on-unit executes a GO TO statement. The following example sets a variable to zero when division by zero occurs.

ON ZERODIVIDE A = 0;

A = X/Y; (If Y equals zero, A is set to zero and execution continues.)

In the following example, a begin block is used to execute several statements when division by zero occurs.

```
ON ZERODIVIDE BEGIN;
PUT DATA(X,Y);
ANS = 0;
IF X = 0 THEN Y = 0;
        ELSE Y = 1;
END;
```

The SNAP option in the ON statement prints relevant error diagnostic information when the condition occurs.

ON ZERODIVIDE SNAP A = 0;

The on-unit in the ON statement can specify SYSTEM to restore the system default for the condition. The following sections describe the system defaults for each condition.

ON FIXEDOVERFLOW SYSTEM;

C. REVERT Statement

The REVERT statement terminates any previous ON statements in the block and reverts to the condition present when the block was entered. The following statement reverts the FIXEDOVERFLOW condition to what it was when the block was entered.

REVERT FIXEDOVERFLOW;

D. SIGNAL Statement

The SIGNAL statement forces a condition to occur, either to invoke the on-unit for testing or to perform the action under program control. The SIGNAL statement invokes the on-unit in somewhat the same way as the CALL statement invokes procedures. The following example forces a CONVERSION condition.

ON CONVERSION PUT DATA(X);

SIGNAL CONVERSION; (Causes PUT DATA(X) to be executed.)

E. Built-in Functions

The following three built-in functions can be used only in an on-unit.

144

1. ONCODE

ONCODE returns an error code as a binary fixed-point integer. The error codes are dependent on the particular compiler implementation.

2. ONLOC

ONLOC returns a varying-length character-string containing the procedure name within which the condition was raised.

3. ONFILE

ONFILE returns a varying-length character-string containing the file-name of the file that caused an input/output or CONVERSION condition to occur.

In the following example, the error code, procedure-name, and file-name associated with the CONVERSION condition are printed.

```
ON CONVERSION BEGIN;
DCL (A,B) CHAR(31) VAR, I DEC(3);
I = ONCODE; A = ONLOC; B = ONFILE;
PUT DATA(I,A,B);
END;
```

F. Computational Conditions

1. CONVERSION (CONV)—Normally enabled

The CONVERSION condition is disabled by NOCONV and enabled by CONV† in a condition-prefix. CONVERSION is an error condition caused by an illegal conversion of character-string data, either internally or in an input/output operation. The ONSOURCE built-in function will return a varying-length character-string containing the string in error. The ONCHAR built-in function will return a fixed-length character-string of length 1 containing the character within the string that caused the error. Both ONSOURCE and ONCHAR can be used only in an on-unit, and both may be used as pseudovariables on the left side of the assignment statement. A statement of the form ONCHAR = 'character'; will replace the character in error with a new character. ONSOURCE = 'string'; replaces the entire string in error with a new character-string. The following example illustrates the use of ONSOURCE and ONCHAR.

```
ON CONV BEGIN;
DCL A CHAR(100) VAR, B CHAR(1);
A = ONSOURCE; B = ONCHAR;
PUT DATA(A,B); (The string, and the character within the string are printed.)
ONCHAR = '0'; (The character in error is replaced with zero.)
END;
```

- Standard action: Print error message and terminate job.
- Results: Undefined.
- Return: To start of character-string and conversion is retried.

2. FIXEDOVERFLOW (FOFL)—Normally enabled

The FIXEDOVERFLOW condition is disabled by NOFOFL and enabled by FOFL in a condition-prefix. FIXEDOVERFLOW is an error condition caused by the length of a fixed-point arithmetic operation exceeding the maximum length allowed (15 for fixed decimal and 31 for binary fixed-point on S/360/370).

† Both the long form and short form may be used; CONV and CONVERSION are identical.

- Standard action: Print error message and terminate job.
- Results: Undefined.
- Return: To point immediately following point of error.

3. OVERFLOW (OFL)—Normally enabled

The OVERFLOW condition is disabled by NOOFL and enabled by OFL in a condition-prefix. OVERFLOW is an error condition caused by the magnitude of a floating-point number exceeding the maximum allowable (10^{75} on S/360/370).

- Standard action: Print error message and terminate job.
- Results: Undefined.
- Return: To point immediately following point of error.

4. UNDERFLOW (UFL)—Normally enabled

The UNDERFLOW condition is disabled by NOUFL and enabled by UFL in a condition-prefix. UNDERFLOW is an error condition caused by the magnitude of a floating-point number becoming smaller than the minimum allowable (10^{-78} on S/360/370) because of an arithmetic operation other than addition or subtraction.

- Standard action: Print error message and continue.
- Results: Set to zero.
- Return: To point immediately following point of error.

5. ZERODIVIDE (ZDIV)—Normally enabled

The ZERODIVIDE condition is disabled by NOZDIV and enabled by ZDIV in a condition-prefix. ZERODIVIDE is an error condition caused by an attempt to divide by zero.

- Standard action: Print error message and terminate job.
- Results: Undefined.
- Return: To point immediately following point of error.

6. SIZE—Normally disabled

The SIZE condition is enabled by SIZE and disabled by NOSIZE in a condition-prefix. SIZE is an error condition caused by the high-order (leftmost) significant binary or decimal digits being lost in an assignment statement or in input/output.

- Standard action: Print error message and terminate job.
- Results: Undefined.
- Return: To point immediately following point of error.

G. Input/Output Conditions

1. ENDPAGE(*file-name*)—Always enabled

ENDPAGE cannot appear in a condition-prefix as it is always enabled. ENDPAGE is caused by a PUT statement for *file-name* when an attempt is made to write a line beyond the limit set for the page size in a PRINT file. The ON statement for ENDPAGE is useful in printing page headings.

- Standard action: Start a new page and continue.
- Results: Line begins on a new page.
- Return: The execution of the PUT statement continues.

2. ENDFILE(*file-name*)—Always enabled

ENDFILE cannot appear in a condition-prefix as it is always enabled. ENDFILE is caused by an attempt to read past the end of file of *file-name* with a GET or READ statement. The ON statement for ENDFILE is used to continue processing after the last record is read from a file.

- Standard action: Print error message and terminate job.
- Results: Null.
- Return: To next statement beyond GET or READ statement.

3. NAME(*file-name*)—Always enabled

NAME cannot appear in a condition-prefix as it is always enabled. NAME is an error condition caused by a variable being read from *file-name* by a data-directed GET statement that is not known within the program. The DATAFIELD built-in function can be used in an on-unit to return a varying-length character-string containing the character stream that caused the error. The following example retrieves any string causing a NAME error on file INPUT and prints it out.

```
ON NAME(INPUT) BEGIN;
DCL A CHAR(80) VAR;
A = DATAFIELD;
PUT DATA(A);
END;
```

- Standard action: Print error message and continue execution.
- Results: Null.
- Return: The next data item in the stream is read.

4. UNDEFINEDFILE(*file-name*)—Always enabled

UNDF cannot appear in a condition-prefix as it is always enabled. UNDEFINEDFILE is an error condition caused by an unsuccessful attempt to open *file-name*.

- Standard action: Print error message and terminate job.
- Results: Null.
- Return: To statement following the statement that attempted to open the file.

5. RECORD(*file-name*)—Always enabled

RECORD cannot appear in a condition-prefix as it is always enabled. RECORD is an error condition caused by a wrong-length record in a READ or WRITE statement for *file-name*; that is, the record size is not equal to the length of the variable being written from or read into.

- Standard action: Print error message and terminate job.
- Results: If the record is longer than the variable, the excess data is lost for a READ, and the excess data is unpredictable for a WRITE. If the record is shorter than the variable, the excess data is not altered for a READ, and the excess data is not transmitted for a WRITE.
- Return: To statement following the READ or WRITE statement.

6. TRANSMIT(*file-name*)—Always enabled

TRANSMIT cannot appear in a condition prefix as it is always enabled. TRANSMIT is an error condition caused by a permanent transmission error on *file-name* during input or output.

- Standard action: Print error message and terminate job.
- Results: Null.
- Return: To point immediately following point of error.

H. Program Checkout Conditions

1. CHECK—Normally disabled

The CHECK condition is enabled by CHECK and disabled by NOCHECK in a condition-prefix. The CHECK condition-prefix traces the flow of execution within a program, and monitors variables as their contents are changed. The CHECK prefix can only be attached to a PROC or BEGIN statement, and it applies to the entire block. The general form is:

(CHECK(*statement-labels, procedure-names, variable-names*)): *label*: *PROC*;

The *statement-labels, procedure-names,* and *variable-names* are all optional and can be listed in any order. As the block is executed, all *statement-labels* and *procedure-names* in the CHECK list are printed as they are encountered. All *variable-names* are printed when their contents are changed, along with their new value. The variable names can be any variable, but not a subscripted array. For example, A is valid as an array, but A(I) is not. In the following statement, the labels A100 and A200 will be printed when execution reaches them. If SQRT is invoked, its name will be printed, and if the values of X or B are changed, their new values are printed.

(CHECK(A100,A200,SQRT,X,B)): COMP: PROC;

CHECK can also appear in an ON statement to allow program action when a CHECK condition occurs.

- Standard action: Print names and values as described above.
- Result: Null.
- Return: To point immediately following point causing condition to occur.

2. CONDITION(*identifier*)—Always enabled

CONDITION cannot appear in a condition-prefix as it is always enabled. CONDITION allows one to set up his or her own conditions and invoke them with the SIGNAL statement. The *identifier* is any PL/I name, and is used to identify the particular CONDITION to be invoked by the SIGNAL statement. The SIGNAL statement is written as:

SIGNAL CONDITION(*identifier*);

CONDITION is generally used in debugging where a BEGIN block prints out several variables, and is invoked by the SIGNAL statement as shown in the following example.

ON CONDITION(PRINT_A_Z) BEGIN;
PUT DATA(A,B,C,D);
IF W = 0 THEN PUT DATA(W,X,Y,Z);
END;

SIGNAL CONDITION(PRINT_A_Z);

- Standard action: Print message and continue execution.
- Results: Null.
- Return: To statement following SIGNAL statement.

3. SUBSCRIPTRANGE (SUBRG)—Normally disabled

The SUBSCRIPTRANGE condition is enabled by SUBRG and disabled by NOSUBRG in a condition-prefix. SUBSCRIPTRANGE is an error condition caused by a subscript in an array variable that is outside the bounds of the array.

- Standard action: Print error message and terminate job.
- Results: Undefined.
- Return: To point immediately following point of error.

4. STRINGRANGE (STRG)—Normally disabled

The STRINGRANGE condition is enabled by STRG and disabled by NOSTRG in a condition-prefix. STRINGRANGE is an error condition caused by the starting position or length arguments in the SUBSTR function being wrong.

- Standard action: Execution continues.
- Results: Null string if length too small; leftmost characters if length too long.
- Return: To point immediately following point of error.

5. STRINGSIZE (STRZ)—Normally disabled

The STRINGSIZE condition is enabled by STRZ and disabled by NOSTRZ in a condition-prefix. STRINGSIZE is a warning condition caused when a string is about to be assigned to a shorter string. STRINGSIZE is not available on all compilers.

- Standard action: Message is printed and execution continues.
- Results: The rightmost bits or characters are truncated to the size of the receiving string.
- Return: To point immediately following point of error.

I. Termination Conditions

1. ERROR—Always enabled

The ERROR condition is caused by any enabled error condition for which an ON condition is not active. These conditions include CONVERSION, FIXEDOVERFLOW, OVER-FLOW, SIZE, ZERODIVIDE, ENDFILE, RECORD, TRANSMIT, UNDEFINEDFILE, and SUBSCRIPTRANGE. The ERROR condition is also caused by any program execution error for which there is no ON condition, such as a memory protection exception. The ERROR condition allows one to program an cn-unit to receive control when any error condition occurs that is not already provided for by other on-units.

- Standard action: Terminate the program.
- Results: None.
- Normal return: To program termination.

2. FINISH—Always enabled

The FINISH condition is caused by the execution of a statement that would cause the program to terminate. The STOP, EXIT, RETURN, and END statements can do this, as can any error condition. The FINISH condition allows one to take special action when a program terminates either normally or abnormally.

- Standard action: Terminate the program.
- Results: None.
- Normal return: To program termination.

IV. EXERCISES

1. Write all the statements available to detect the possible errors in the following statement.

$$K = ((B**N)/D)*(I(L)*J) \qquad\qquad K = ((B**N)/D)*(I(L)*J);$$

2. Read in a complete file, terminating after reading the end-of-file and print the number of records read on the operator's console. Each record contains 80 characters. If a transmission error occurs, display the record number on the operator's console and await a response from him.

3. (PL/I only). Two variables are defined as follows:

DCL A FIXED(5), B CHAR(5);

Write the statements necessary to detect and correct any conversion error in the following assignment statement. Display any illegal characters and set them to zero to enable the conversion to continue.

A = B;

4. (PL/I only). The following statement appears within a program:

READ FILE(PAYROLL) INTO (CURRENT);

Write all the statements available to detect the possible errors that can occur during execution of the statement.

5. (PL/I only). Assume that a main program named COMPUTE has been written. Write the debugging statements necessary to display the labels START, READ_MORE, and ALL_DONE whenever they are encountered. Also print the name of the SQRT and SUBSTR built-in functions when they are invoked. Display the contents of the variable MAX and the array VALUES whenever they are changed. Print an error message if an array is referenced with incorrect subscript. Ignore any underflow error conditions.

Chapter 12

Special PL/I Language Features

The PL/I language features described in this chapter are not available in FORTRAN. Data structures and the picture-specification are familiar to all COBOL programmers, and are very useful. The compile-time facilities, list processing, multitasking, and recursion all have more specialized uses, and they are not likely to be required for most programming tasks. This chapter examines the special features only briefly, and is intended to give a flavor of their usage, rather than provide an exhaustive description.

I. DATA STRUCTURES

A. Declaration of Structures

Data structures, also a basic part of the COBOL language, are as important in business applications as arrays are in scientific applications. A data structure is a hierarchical collection of related data items, which may be of different data types. For example, a structure describing a person might include the person's name and date of birth. Some items might themselves be substructures, as for example the date of birth which consists of a month, a day, and a year. The following example shows how such a data structure is defined in PL/I.

```
DCL 1 PERSON,
      2 NAME CHAR(25),
      2 BIRTH_DATE,
        3 MONTH CHAR(9),
        3 DAY FIXED(2),
        3 YEAR FIXED(4);
```

The indentation of the levels makes them easier to read, but as with all PL/I statements, they could all have been written on the same line. The structure name, PERSON in the example above must be level 1, and all succeeding substructures must have levels greater than 1. The level numbers need not be consecutive, as they serve only to indicate the relative hierarchy of the structure. For example, the following structure is identical to the one above.

```
DCL 1 PERSON, 4 NAME CHAR(25), 4 BIRTH_DATE, 10 MONTH CHAR(9),
                                  10 DAY FIXED(2), 10 YEAR FIXED(4);
```

Only the lowest element in the structure hierarchy can contain data. In the above structure, neither PERSON nor BIRTH_DATE can contain data because they have data elements defined below them. The entire structure is referred to by its name, for example, PERSON in the example above. Substructures and elements are referred to by *qualifying* the name. This is done by writing each name in the hierarchy, from highest to lowest, separated by periods. For example, PERSON.NAME refers to the person's name, PERSON.BIRTH_DATE refers to the birth date substructure, and PERSON.BIRTH_DATE.MONTH refers to the month of the person's birth. Names need to be qualified only with enough higher levels to make them unique. This is illustrated by the following two structures.

```
DCL 1 A,                        DCL 1 J,
    2 B,                            2 K,
        3 V FIXED(3),                   3 X FIXED(3),
        3 W FIXED(3),                   3 W FIXED(3),
    2 C,                                3 Z FIXED(3),
        3 X FIXED(3),               2 C,
        3 Y FIXED(3),                   3 Y FIXED(3),
        3 Z FIXED(3);                   3 Z FIXED(3);
```

The name B is unique and can be written as B or A.B. The name V is unique and can be written as V, B.V. A.V. or A.B.V. The name W is not unique, and must be written as B.W, A.W, or A.B.W to identify the W in the A structure.

A second structure can be defined to be identical to all or parts of another structure by using the LIKE attribute on the DCL statement. The form is:

DCL *name* LIKE *structure*;

All substructures below the named *structure* are copied, along with their attributes. The following examples declare structures like those previously defined.

```
DCL 1 STORAGE LIKE A;      Results in:      DCL 1 STORAGE,
                                                2 B,
                                                    3 V FIXED(3),
                                                    3 W FIXED(3),
                                                2 C,
                                                    3 X FIXED(3),
                                                    3 Y FIXED(3),
                                                    3 Z FIXED(3);
DCL 1 BERG LIKE J.C;       Results in:      DCL 1 BERG,
                                                3 Y FIXED(3),
                                                3 Z FIXED(3);
```

The LIKE structure cannot itself be defined LIKE another.

```
DCL 1 A,   1 B LIKE A,   1 C LIKE B;   (Wrong!)
DCL 1 A,   1 B LIKE A,   1 C LIKE A;   (Correct)
```

No dimensions of the named structure are copied, but any dimensions below it are.

```
DCL 1 MAX(3),
    2 WEIGHT(2),
        3 LBS FIXED(5),
        3 OUNCES FIXED(5),
    2 HEIGHT FIXED(5);
DCL 1 MIN LIKE MAX;        Results in:      DCL 1 MIN,
                                                2 WEIGHT(2),
                                                    3 LBS FIXED(5),
                                                    3 OUNCES FIXED(5),
                                                2 HEIGHT FIXED(5);
```

DCL 1 HEAVY(6) LIKE MAX.WEIGHT;

	Results in:	DCL 1 HEAVY(6),
		3 LBS FIXED(5),
		3 OUNCES FIXED(5);

B. Structure Operations

Structures and substructures named in expressions are operated on element-by-element. For example, if a number is added to a structure, it is added to all elements of the structure, and if two structures are added together, each consecutive element is added, regardless of its name or the substructure within which it lies. If the corresponding elements are of a different data type, conversion will occur. All structures in an expression must have the same number of elements. Array expressions are not permitted in combination with structure expressions.

In the following example, the structures A and J defined previously in this section appear in the following assignment statements.

A = J + 1;	Results in:	A.B.V = J.K.X + 1;
		A.B.W = J.K.W + 1;
		A.C.X = J.K.Z + 1;
		A.C.Y = J.C.Y + 1;
		A.C.Z = J.C.Z + 1;
A.C = J.K;	Results in:	A.C.X = J.K.X;
		A.C.Y = J.K.W;
		A.C.Z = J.K.Z;

The BY NAME clause appended to the end of the assignment statement causes only elements whose qualified names are the same to participate in the operation.

A = J + 1, BY NAME;	Results in:	A.C.Y = J.C.Y + 1;
		A.C.Z = J.C.Z + 1;
A.B = J.K, BY NAME;	Results in:	A.B.W = J.K.W;

The IF statement can test only elements of a structure. It cannot test entire structures or substructures.

C. Structure Arrays

Structures and substructures can also be defined as arrays. The following structure defines 50 states, 5 rivers within each state, 20 counties within each state, and 10 cities within each county.

```
DCL 1 STATE(50),        (50 states)
       2 NAME CHAR(25),        (name of state)
       2 RIVER(5) CHAR(25),        (5 rivers per state)
       2 COUNTY(20),        (20 counties per state)
         3 CITY(10),        (10 cities per county)
           4 NAME CHAR(25),        (name of city)
           4 SIZE FIXED;        (size of city)
```

The subscripts of structure arrays are written either after each name or at the end of all names; for example, STATE(6).COUNTY(3).CITY(4).NAME or STATE.COUNTY.CITY.NAME(6,3,4).

Structure arrays cannot appear in array expressions.

```
    STATE.SIZE = 0; (Wrong! Must be written as follows:)
LOOP: DO I = 1 TO 50;
      DO J = 1 TO 20;
      DO K = 1 TO 10;
      STATE.COUNTY.CITY.SIZE(I,J,K) = 0;
      END LOOP;
```

D. Exercises

1. Two structures are defined as follows:
```
   DCL 1 ONE,
        2 A(3),
          3 B CHAR(3),
          3 C FIXED(3),
          3 D,
            4 E FLOAT(6),
            4 F CHAR(2),
        2 G CHAR(6),
        2 H LIKE ONE.G;
   DCL 1 TWO,
        2 P(3),
          3 D CHAR(3),
          3 C FIXED(3),
          3 Q LIKE ONE.D,
        2 R CHAR(6),
        2 S LIKE ONE.G;
```

Note the elements that participate in the following statements.

(a) ONE = TWO;
(b) ONE = TWO, BY NAME;
(c) ONE.A(1) = P(1), BY NAME;
(d) G = S;
(e) H = P.D(1) ∥ P.Q(1);

2. Define a structure that contains a four-digit project number, a 25-character name, and an overhead percentage in decimal fixed-point of precision (6,2). Read in a file of such records using unformatted I/O, and print the number of duplicate project numbers. Assume that the file is in sort by project number.

II. PICTURE-SPECIFICATION

The picture-specification has no counterpart in FORTRAN, but is familiar to all COBOL programmers. The picture-specification allows editing of data items, such as omitting or including leading zeros, inserting commas and decimal points, and preceding the number with a $ sign. The picture-specification is especially useful with unformatted I/O. Data is stored in character form already formatted, and no conversion is required to print it. This allows the use of the more efficient unformatted I/O to print reports; something not possible in FORTRAN. The picture-specification is written as follows in the DCL statement as a data type.

DCL *name* PICTURE '*picture-specification*';

PICTURE is usually written in its short form as PIC. The P format-item written as P'*picture-specification*' can also appear in edit-directed format-lists. The *picture-specification* consists of a group of edit characters that specify the size of the field and the editing to be done on it.

DCL SIZE PIC '999V999';

Edit characters that are coded several times may be preceded by a repetition factor enclosed in parentheses.

DCL SIZE PIC '(4)Z9V(5)9'; is the same as DCL SIZE PIC 'ZZZZ9V99999';

There are two types of picture-specifications: character and numeric.

A.   Character Picture-specification

Character picture-specifications are used to store character data in which only certain types of characters may appear in specified positions. The character picture-specification can contain only the following edit characters.

A Alphabetic characters (A to Z, \$, @, #) or blank.
9 Numeric characters (0 to 9) or blank.
X Any characters.

If an attempt is made to store a character in a character variable not allowed by the edit character, the CONVERSION condition described in Chapter 11 is raised.

DCL A PIC '99';   (A can contain only numeric characters.)
DCL B PIC '9A';   (B can contain only numeric characters in the first position, and any character in the second position.)
DCL C PIC 'XX';   (C can contain any two characters. This is identical to DCL C CHAR(2);)
DCL D PIC 'A999';   (D can contain only alphabetic characters in the first position, and only numeric characters in the second, third, and fourth positions.)

B.   Numeric Picture-specification

Picture data is stored in character form, and is converted to fixed decimal for arithmetic operations. Its primary use is for printing numbers as it is more efficient for I/O than it is for computations. If there are many arithmetic computations, it is more efficient to use fixed-point decimal numbers and then store the results in the PICTURE item just prior to printing. The following edit characters may appear in numeric picture-specifications.

1.   9 (Decimal digit). The 9 edit character in a picture-specification represents a decimal digit (0 to 9) within the number. Each 9 occupies a character position. Signs are not printed.

DCL A PIC '9999';   (The variable A occupies four character positions.)
A = 2;   (A contains '0002')

155

2. V (Decimal alignment). A single V edit character can be coded in a picture-specification to indicate the position of the internal decimal point. V is not stored as a character, and does not occupy a character position.

DCL A PIC '999V99';   (The variable A has precision (5,2), and occupies five character positions)

A = 2.3;   (A contains '00230')

3. Z (Leading zero suppression). The Z edit character is similar to the 9 edit character, except that it replaces leading zeros with blanks. Z cannot appear to the right of a 9 edit character.

DCL A PIC 'ZZ9V99';

A = 2.31;   (A contains 'bb231')
A = 26.2;   (A contains 'b2620')
A = .94;   (A contains 'bb094')

4. * (Leading asterisks). The * edit character is identical to the Z edit character, but it replaces leading zeros with asterisks rather than blanks. It cannot appear in the same picture-specification as the Z; nor can it appear to the right of a 9 edit character.

DCL A PIC '**9V99';
A = 26.31;   (A contains '*2631')

5. Y (Zero suppression). The Y edit character causes any zero digit, leading or nonleading, to be replaced by a blank. It differs from the Z in that it can appear to the right of a 9 edit character.

DCL A PIC 'YY9VYY';
A = 2.2;   (A contains 'bb22b')

6. . (Decimal point). The decimal point edit character is inserted just as it appears in the picture-specification, and it occupies a character position. It is independent of the internal decimal point specified by the V edit character, but is normally coded along with the V. If it is coded n positions to the left of the V, it has the effect of scaling the printed number by 10^{-n}; placing it n positions to the right of the V scales the number by 10^n.

DCL A PIC 'ZZ9V.99';
A = 22.31;   (A contains 'b22.31')

7. , (Comma). The comma edit character is inserted just as it appears in the picture-specification, and it counts as a character position. If leading zeros are suppressed, the comma is replaced by a blank (or asterisk if * is coded rather than Z) if all the characters to the left of the comma are zero.

DCL A PIC '9,999';
A = 4;   (A contains '0,004')
A = 4000;   (A contains '4,000')
DCL B PIC 'Z,ZZ9';
B = 4;   (B contains 'bbbb4')
B = 4000;   (B contains '4,000')

8. / (Slash). The / edit character is identical to the comma, except that a / is inserted in the field.

DCL A PIC '99/99';
A = 250;   (A contains '02/50')

9. B (Blank). The B edit character causes a blank to be inserted wherever it appears in a picture-specification, and it counts as a character position.

DCL A PIC 'B99B';
A = 21;   (A contains 'b21b')

10. $ (Dollar sign). The $ edit character is inserted just as it appears in the picture-specification, and it counts as a character position. A series of $'s suppress leading zeros in the same manner as the Z edit character, and a single $ is inserted to the left of the first nonzero digit.

DCL A PIC '$999';
A = 4;   (A contains '$004')
DCL B PIC '$$$9';
B = 4;   (B contains 'bb$4')

11. S (Sign). The S edit character specifies that the sign (+ or −) be printed just as it appears in the picture-specification, and it counts as a character position. A series of S's suppress leading zeros in the same manner as the Z edit character, and the sign is inserted to the left of the first nonzero digit.

DCL A PIC 'S999';
A = −2;   (A contains '−002')
DCL B PIC 'SSS9';
B = 2;   (B contains 'bb+2')

12. − (Minus sign). The minus sign edit character is identical to the S edit character, but only minus signs are inserted. Positive numbers are unsigned.

DCL A PIC '−−−9';
A = −2;   (A contains 'bb−2')
A = 2;   (A contains 'bbb2')

13. + (Plus sign). The plus sign edit character is identical to the S edit character, but only plus signs are inserted. Negative numbers are unsigned.

DCL A PIC '+999';
A = 2;   (A contains '+002')
A = −2;   (A contains '0002')

14. CR (Credit symbol). The CR edit character is printed just as it appears if the number is negative; otherwise it is replaced by two blanks. CR counts as two character positions.

DCL A PIC '999CR';
A = −27;   (A contains '027CR')
A = 27;   (A contains '027bb')

15. DB (Debit symbol). The DB edit character is identical to the CR edit character, except that DB is printed if the number is negative.

```
DCL A PIC 'DB99';
A = −1;        (A contains 'DB01')
A = 1;         (A contains 'bb01')
```

C. Exercises

1. Show what the following numbers will be converted to if processed by the corresponding format items.

Picture	Numbers	
(3)9V.9	264.7	0.3
(2)Y9VYYY	126.4	33.424
/B*V*9/	0.01	1.1
(3)$,$$9V.99CR	−1.1	10429.64
$(3)Z,ZZZV.ZZ	120514.21	77.4
$−−−−9V.99	−133.25	23.98
(4)9V99.9	5430.234	823.984

2. Print a table of the squares of the integers from 1 to 1000 formatted as shown. Print 50 values per page. Use structures and unformatted I/O to print the table.

```
            SQUARES OF NUMBERS                    PAGE xxx
            NUMBER        SQUARE
               1             1
               2             4
               :             :
             1000        1,000,000
```

3. Print a table showing the future value of an amount invested at 8% per annum in increments of 1 year for 30 years. The equation for the future value is: $amount(1.08)^n$, where n is the year. Use data structures and unformatted I/O to print the table in the format shown below. Print the table for amounts ranging from $100 to $1000 in increments of $200.

```
        FUTURE VALUE TABLE                              PAGE xxx
        AMOUNT: $100.00              INTEREST RATE: 8.00%
            YEAR                        FUTURE VALUE
             1                             $108.00
             2                             $116.64
             :                                :
             30                           $1,006.27
```

III. COMPILE-TIME FACILITIES

The compile-time facilities of PL/I direct the compiler on operations to be performed on the source statements before they are compiled. Names within a program can be changed, source statements from a library can be included, statements can be generated, and selected portions of the program can be included or excluded from the compilation.

The ability to include source statements from a library is perhaps the most useful facility, and is especially important in copying data structures that describe common files. This facility is functionally the same as the COPY feature in the COBOL language. The ability to generate instructions or selectively compile portions of a program resembles the macro facility of assembler languages.

The compile-time statements are interspersed with the normal statements, and are preceded by a percent sign (%). They resemble the normal PL/I statements, and consist of the %DCL, %assignment, %DO, %END, %IF, %GO TO, %null, and the %PROC statement. Two additional statements, the %DEACTIVATE and the %ACTIVATE, deactivate and activate names that are being changed within a program.

A preprocessor pass is first made through the program to do all operations specified by the compile-time statements. A second pass is then made to do the actual compilation on the changed program. The compile-time statements have no affect during the compilation, but only during the preprocessor pass. The compile-time facility increases compilation time and is likely to be quite compiler dependent. The following brief description is for S/360/370.

A. Inclusion of Statements from a Library—%INCLUDE

The %INCLUDE statement names a library from which to copy source statements. The statements are copied into the program at the point where the %INCLUDE statement is placed. The general form of the %INCLUDE statement is:

> %INCLUDE ddname(membername),ddname(membername),...

The *ddname* is the name of the S/360/370 Job Control Language DD card that describes the library. The *ddname* can be omitted, and the SYSLIB DD card is assumed for the *ddname*. The *membername* is the name of the member within the library to copy. Several members can be copied into the program from one or more libraries. If %INCLUDE statements are copied from a library, they in turn will cause members to be brought in from a library. In the following example, a %INCLUDE statement is used to include source statements.

> DCL A FIXED;
> %INCLUDE LIB(FILE); (Statements contained in the FILE member are inserted
> here.)
>
> DCL B FIXED;

//PLIL.LIB DD DSN = SUBLIB,DISP = SHR,...   (The LIB card describes the library
from which to copy the member FILE.)

The compile-time facility must be requested in S/360/370 on the EXEC Job Control Language card as follows:

// EXEC PL1LCLG,PARM.PL1F = 'MACRO'

B. Declaration of Preprocessor Variables—%DCL

Names within a PL/I program to be operated on by the preprocessor must first be declared in a %DCL statement. The data types FIXED or CHAR must be specified, with no other attributes. FIXED names can be replaced with decimal fixed-point numbers of precision (5,0). CHAR names can be replaced by varying-length character-strings of any length. The following statements declare A, B, and TIME_OF_DAY as preprocessor variables.

> %DCL A FIXED, B CHAR;
> %DCL TIME_OF_DAY CHAR;

C. Changing Names—%*assignment*

Once a preprocessor variable has been declared, the %*assignment* statement can change the name wherever it appears within the program, either as a label, a variable, or as a PL/I key word. The name is not changed if it appears in comments or in character-string constants. In the following example, the name STATE is changed to CITY, and the name SIZE is changed to 2000.

%DCL STATE CHAR, SIZE FIXED;   (STATE and SIZE are declared to be active as preprocessor variables.)

%STATE = 'CITY';   (The name STATE will be changed to CITY wherever it appears following this statement in the program.)

%SIZE = 2000;   (The name SIZE is changed to the number 2000.)

DCL STATE FIXED;   (Changed to DCL CITY FIXED;)
STATE = SIZE;   (Changed to CITY = 2000;)
STATE_REV(SIZE) = 'STATE TAX' ‖ STATE;
    (Changed to STATE_REV(2000) = 'STATE TAX' ‖ CITY; STATE_REV is not changed because STATE is active only for complete names, not parts of names. 'STATE TAX' is not changed because character-string constants are not changed.)

Preprocessor expressions in the %*assignment* statement and in other preprocessor statements are written and evaluated as normal PL/I statements with the following restrictions. Operands can consist only of preprocessor variables, decimal fixed-point, bit-string, or character-string constants, the built-in function SUBSTR, and references to preprocessor procedures. Only decimal fixed-point arithmetic of precision (5,0) is performed in arithmetic operations, and the exponentiation symbol (**) cannot be used. When decimal fixed-point numbers are converted to character-strings, the result is a character-string of length 9, with leading zeros replaced by blanks.

Values assigned to preprocessor variables can themselves be preprocessor variables as shown in the following example.

%DCL A CHAR, B FIXED;   (A and B are declared as preprocessor variables.)
%A = 'B/C';   (The name A is set to B/C.)
%B = 100;   (The name B is set to 100.)

Y = A;   (A is first changed to B/C, and B is then changed to 100. The result is Y = 100/C;)

D. Deactivating and Activating Names—%DEACTIVATE, %ACTIVATE

The %DEACTIVATE statement deactivates a name so that it is not changed by the compile-time facility, and the %ACTIVATE statement reactivates it. (The %DCL statement initially activates the name.) The following example deactivates two names and reactivates one of them.

%DCL A CHAR, B CHAR;   (A and B are declared to be preprocessor variables.)
%A = 'FIRST'; %B = 'POST';   (A and B are assigned values.)

A = B;   (Changed to FIRST = POST;)
%DEACTIVATE A,B;   (A and B are deactivated.)
C = A/B;   (Statement is not changed.)
%ACTIVATE B;   (B is activated.)
E = A + B;   (Changed to E = A + POST;)

E. Preprocessor Control Statements: %null, %GO TO, %DO, %END, %IF

The preprocessor control statements direct the flow of processing to include or exclude statements from compilation, and to generate statements.

1. *%null.* The *%null* statement is used either to provide a target for a label in a %GO TO statement, or in the THEN or ELSE clauses of the %IF statement. The *%null* statement is written as:

%label: ;

2. %GO TO. All preprocessor statements can have labels, and the %GO TO transfers control to such a label. Compilation follows the flow of control set by the %GO TO statement. Labels on preprocessor statements must be preceded by the percent symbol. For example, *%label*: ACTIVATE. The following example illustrates the use of the %GO TO statement.

```
        %GO TO PART1;
        A = 10; B = 6;
%PART1: GO TO PART3;
%PART2: ;
        E = 1; F = 2;
        %GO TO DONE;
%PART3: ;
        C = 3;
        %GO TO PART2;
%DONE: ;
```

The statements above are compiled as:

```
C = 3;
E = 1; F = 2;
```

3. %DO, %END. The %DO statement can be written in only one form as 'DO $i = m1$ TO $m2$ BY $m3$;' The following example illustrates its use in generating multiple statements.

```
%DCL I FIXED;
%GEN_LOOP: DO I = 1 TO 3;
            A(I) = B(I) + C(4−I);
            %END GEN_LOOP;
```

The following three statements are generated for compilation.

```
A(1) = B(1) + C(3);
A(2) = B(2) + C(2);
A(3) = B(3) + C(1);
```

4. %IF. The %IF statement is similar to the normal IF statement, and is written as follows:

%IF *pre-processor expression* %THEN %*pre-processor clause*;
%ELSE %*pre-processor clause*;

The following example generates the three statements above, using the %IF.

```
%DCL I FIXED;
%I = 1;
%START: ;
        A(I) = B(I) + C(4 − I);
        %I = I + 1;
        %IF I < 4 %THEN %GO TO START;
```

F.   Preprocessor Procedure Functions: %PROC, %END

The %PROC statement allows preprocessor function procedures to be written to be invoked when a name corresponding to the procedure name is encountered. The function returns a single value to replace the name. Preprocessor functions must begin with a %PROC statement and end with a %END statement. The statements within preprocessor functions are normal PL/I statements, not preprocessor statements, and cannot have a leading % symbol. As with normal functions, preprocessor functions can have arguments. The general form of the %PROC statement is:

%*label*: PROC (*argument list, if any*) RETURNS(FIXED *or* CHAR);

Names used to invoke preprocessor functions must be declared as ENTRY in a %DCL statement. The %DCL statement is written as:

%DCL *name* ENTRY (*data type* CHAR *or* FIXED *for each argument*)
RETURNS(CHAR *or* FIXED);

The following preprocessor function is written to change the name of array CITY_BY_STATE to STATE_BY_CITY, and to reverse the order of the two subscripts wherever the array appears in the program. For example, CITY_BY_STATE(2,10) would be changed to STATE_BY_CITY(10,2). The procedure is written as follows:

```
%CITY_BY_STATE: PROC(I,J) RETURNS(CHAR);
        DCL (I,J) CHAR(5);
        RETURN('STATE_BY_CITY(' ‖ J ‖ ',' ‖ I ‖ ')');
        %END CITY_BY_STATE;
```

The %DCL statement must then declare CITY_BY_STATE as an entry, and any reference to the array name invokes the function to change the array name and reverse its arguments.

%DCL CITY_BY_STATE ENTRY(CHAR,CHAR) RETURNS(CHAR);
Y = CITY_BY_STATE(2,8);   (Changed to Y = STATE_BY_CITY(8,2);)

G. Exercises

1. It is desired to convert all single-precision floating-point numbers in a PL/I program to FIXED BIN(31). Assume that all single-precision variables appear in DCL statements as FLOAT. Write the preprocessor statements necessary to make the conversion.

2. A one-dimensional array named MAX must be declared as FIXED DEC(2). It must also be initialized with each successive 10 elements of the array assigned the values 1 to 10, that is, MAX(1) = 1, MAX(2) = 2,..., MAX(10) = 10, MAX(11) = 1,..., MAX(20) = 10, MAX(21) = 1. Write the preprocessor statements necessary to create the required DCL statement, and allow the size of the array to vary, depending on a value assigned to a preprocessor variable named SIZE. Assign a value of 100 to SIZE.

3. A two-dimensional array named SIZE has dimensions of (6,8). Change SIZE to a one-dimensional array with dimension of (48), mapping the subscripts as follows:

Old SIZE	New SIZE
SIZE(1,1)	SIZE(1)
SIZE(1,2)	SIZE(2)
$\vdots$	$\vdots$
SIZE(1,8)	SIZE(8)
SIZE(2,1)	SIZE(9)
SIZE(2,2)	SIZE(10)
$\vdots$	$\vdots$
SIZE(6,8)	SIZE(48)

Assume that SIZE is indexed only by integer constants. Write the preprocessor statements necessary to make the changes. Hint—use a preprocessor function.

4. The following statements must be generated within a program:

V1(1) = V1(1)/W(10);
V2(10) = V2(10)/W(11);
V1(2) = V1(2)/W(9);
V2(9) = V2(9)/W(12);
    $\vdots$
V1(10) = V1(10)/W(1);
V2(1) = V2(1)/W(20);

Write the preprocessor statements necessary to generate the statements above.

IV. LIST PROCESSING

PL/I list processing provides several facilities normally found only in assembler languages, or in specialized list-processing languages. The essence of list processing is the ability to dynamically allocate blocks of core storage, link these blocks together into a structure, and store and retrieve data from the blocks. This is done in PL/I by dynamically allocating blocks of core storage similar to the manner in which controlled storage, described in Chapter 7, is allocated, and then retrieving the core storage address of each block for use in linking the blocks together and as a reference for storing and retrieving data from the blocks.

List processing is often required for complicated data structures, such as tree or ring structures, that are either very difficult or impossible to achieve with arrays or other normal means. List processing is also required for many on-line applications in which a data structure is constantly changed in real time, and recreating the entire structure for each change is too inefficient.

As an example of a simple list-processing structure, assume that a file contains the names of people, one per record, in random order, and that a structure is to be created to place the names in alphabetic order. It is not known how many people are in the file, and so a new block of storage is allocated for each person when a record is read in. Each block of storage points to the next block in alphabetic order, and so to place a person in sequence, only the appropriate pointers need to be changed. The following diagram shows the structure as it might appear after three names are read in. The individual blocks of storage are not necessarily contiguous, but could be scattered over core.

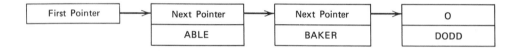

If the next name read in is BISHOP, storage would be allocated for it, and it would be placed in alphabetic order by searching down the list until a name is encountered that is alphabetically greater than it is; DODD is this case. When found, the pointers are revised. BISHOP's position is made to point to DODD, and BAKER's pointer is made to point to BISHOP. The structure then looks as follows:

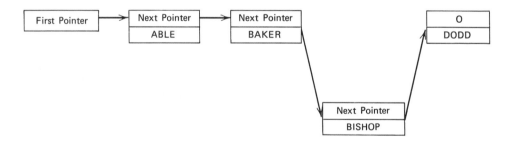

Individual blocks of list-processing storage are called *based-variables*, and they are usually defined as data structures. Based-variables must be declared in a DCL statement. Storage is then allocated by the ALLOCATE statement, and released by the FREE statement in the same way in which controlled storage is allocated and released. Since several based-variables with identical structures can exist at one time, a *pointer-variable* is required to point to a specific one. The ALLOCATE statement stores the address of the based-variable in a pointer-variable when storage is allocated. Then to refer to a specific based-variable, the name is qualified by the pointer-variable that contains its address. The qualification is written as:

pointer-variable − > based-variable

The $->$ symbol is composed of a minus sign $(-)$ and the greater than symbol $(>)$. A default pointer-variable is declared for the based-variable in the DCL statement, and if the based-variable name is not qualified, the default pointer-variable automatically qualifies it.

A. DCL Statement for Based- and Pointer-Variables

The DCL statement defines the based-variable and assigns a default pointer-variable to it. The form is:

DCL *based-variable* BASED (*pointer-variable*) *attributes*;

Based-variables cannot be given EXTERNAL, VARYING, or INITIAL attributes in the DCL statement. The following example creates a simple based-variable structure named CITY.

DCL 1 CITY BASED (THIS),
    2 NEXT POINTER,
    2 SIZE FIXED(10);

THIS is defined as the default pointer-variable for CITY. CITY has two data elements, a SIZE, and a pointer-variable named NEXT. Pointer-variables such as NEXT can be declared as a data type in a DCL statement. The form is:

DCL *pointer-variable* POINTER;

Pointer-variables can receive only the value of another pointer-variable in an assignment statement, and they can be operated upon only the equal $(=)$ or not equal $(\neg =)$ operations. The following statement declares FIRST to be a pointer-variable.

DCL FIRST POINTER;

B. ALLOCATE Statement for Based-Variables

Storage is allocated for pointer-variables by the ALLOCATE statement as follows:

ALLOCATE *based-variable*;   (The address of the *based-variable* is stored in the default pointer-variable.)
ALLOCATE *based-variable* SET (*pointer-variable*);   (The address of the *based-variable* is stored in the *pointer-variable*.)

The following example allocates two blocks of storage for the above based-variable CITY.

ALLOCATE CITY SET(FIRST);   (The address is stored in FIRST.)
ALLOCATE CITY;   (The address is stored in the default pointer-variable THIS.)

The first CITY is referred to by FIRST $->$ CITY, and the second city is referred to by either CITY or THIS $->$ CITY. The two based-variables can now be linked together by storing the pointer to the second CITY into the first CITY.

FIRST $->$ CITY.NEXT = THIS;

A special built-in function called NULL can be stored in a pointer-variable to terminate a chain.

THIS $->$ CITY.NEXT = NULL;

The structure now looks as follows:

A simple loop can be written to set the size of each city to zero, regardless of the number of cities linked together.

```
DCL TEMP POINTER;  (Declare TEMP as a pointer-variable.)
TEMP = FIRST;        (Set TEMP to point to the first city.)
DO WHILE TEMP ¬ = NULL;        (Loop until no more cities.)
TEMP − >CITY.SIZE = 0;        (Set the city size to zero.)
TEMP = TEMP − >CITY.NEXT;        (Get the pointer to the next city.)
END;
```

The default pointer-variable can save coding. The following loop is identical to the above.

```
THIS = FIRST;
LOOP: CITY.SIZE = 0;
        THIS = CITY.NEXT;
        IF THIS ¬ = NULL THEN GO TO LOOP;
```

A third city can be created and inserted between the first and second cities.

```
ALLOCATE CITY SET TEMP;        (Create the third city.)
TEMP − >CITY.NEXT = FIRST − >CITY.NEXT;        (The third city points to
                                                     the second city.)
FIRST − >CITY.NEXT = TEMP;        (The first city points to the third city.)
```

The structure now looks as follows:

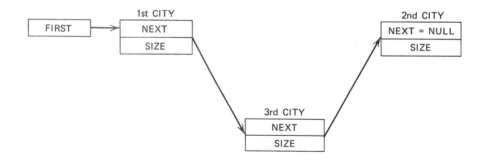

C.   FREE Statement for Based-Variables

The FREE statement releases based-variable storage. FREE has two forms as follows:

FREE *based-variable*;   (The *based-variable* pointed to by the default pointer-variable is released.)

FREE *pointer-variable* − >*based-variable*;   (The *based-variable* pointed to by the *pointer-variable* is released.)

The following loop releases storage for all of the above cities. The default pointer-variable is used for convenience.

```
THIS = FIRST;        (Get the address of the first city.)
DO WHILE FIRST ¬= NULL;        (Loop until no more cities.)
FIRST = CITY.NEXT;        (Save the address of the next city.)
FREE CITY;        (Release storage for this city.)
END;
```

D.   ADDR Built-in Function

The ADDR built-in function retrieves the address of nonbased-variables. The following example shows the form of the ADDR function.

```
DCL P POINTER;        (P is declared as a pointer.)
P = ADDR(Z);        (The address of Z is stored in P.)
P = ADDR(X(10,2));        (The address of element (10,2) in array X is stored in P.)
P = ADDR(X);        (The address of element (1,1) in array X is stored in P.)
```

A based-variable structure may be defined, and then effectively made equivalent to a non-based-variable with a different structure by referencing the based-variable with the nonbased-variable address. The following example illustrates this.

```
DCL 1 FORM;        (Structure FORM is a normal structure)
     2 SIZE FIXED BIN(31),        (SIZE is an integer)
     2 HEIGHT FLOAT(6);        (HEIGHT is floating-point)
DCL 1 MASS BASED(PTR),        (Structure MASS is a based-variable with PTR as
                                        its pointer-variable)
     2 SIZE FLOAT(6),        (SIZE is floating-point)
     2 HEIGHT FIXED BIN(31);        (HEIGHT is an integer)
PTR = ADDR(FORM);        (The address of FORM is stored in PTR)
```

At this point, FORM.SIZE is considered an integer, and PTR − >MASS.SIZE is considered a floating-point number, when in fact they both refer to the same core storage location and are equivalent.

E.   Manipulation of Input/Output Buffers

The READ statement can set a pointer-variable to the address of a record in an input buffer. This allows data within a buffer to be manipulated after a record is read. The form is:

```
READ FILE(file-name) SET (pointer-variable);
```

The LOCATE statement allocates a based-variable within an output buffer, and returns the address. This allows data to be stored directly into an output buffer. A subsequent LOCATE or CLOSE statement transmits the record, and no READ is required. The two forms are:

```
LOCATE based-variable FILE (file-name);        (The address is stored in the default
                                                        pointer-variable.)
LOCATE based-variable FILE (file-name) SET (pointer-variable);        (The address is
                                                        stored in the pointer-variable.)
```

F.   Other Facilities

The size of a based-variable array can be set when the based-variable is allocated, and the size then stored in the based-variable structure, making the array self-defining. Based-variables can also be allocated in specific areas of core storage, and referred to by their relative position (called an *offset*) as a pointer rather than the absolute core address. This allows the data to be written out and read back in at a later time into a different part of core without destroying the validity of the pointer-variables. (In modern multiprogramming systems, a job will likely occupy different areas of core storage each time it runs, and this would make any previous absolute core addresses useless.)

G.   Exercises

1.   The following structure is defined.

```
DCL 1 FORM,
      2 FLAG CHAR(1),
      2 NUMBER CHAR(4),
      2 AMOUNT CHAR(4),
      2 TIME CHAR(4);
```

Assume that a file named TEST is to be read into FORM with unformatted I/O. If FORM. FLAG equals '1' the data is in character form corresponding to the structure. If FORM.FLAG equals '2', NUMBER, AMOUNT, and TIME are all FLOAT(6), each occupying four bytes each. If FORM.FLAG equals '3', NUMBER, AMOUNT, and TIME are all FIXED BIN(31), each occupying four bytes each. Using based-variables, redefine the array so that it can be properly manipulated. Write a program to read in the file with unformatted I/O and print out its contents using edit-directed output.

2.   Store the integers from 1 to 100 in based-variables, one based-variable per number. Link the based-variables together, and then write the necessary statements to free all of the based-variables.

3.   A file containing 80-column card images is to be read in. Columns 1 to 10 contain a single integer number. The size of the file is unknown.

- Read in the entire file and store all of the numbers in ascending order using based-variables.
- After the file is read in, eliminate all numbers with an absolute magnitude greater than 400.

V.   MULTITASKING

Multitasking is the ability to perform several concurrent tasks within a program. For example, a program might initiate a task to write a message to the operator and await a response. The main program could then continue on, and later check to see if the operator has responded. Multitasking is generally required only for specialized real-time applications in which a program must respond to many asynchronous requests. Multitasking can also be used in some cases to increase the efficiency of a program by overlapping central processing unit operations with I/O operations. However, most operating systems execute several entire programs concurrently. Thus while it may be efficient for a single program running by itself to balance CPU and I/O operations, the effect is lost when several programs are run concurrently, and it may actually degrade overall performance because of the additional overhead required for multitasking.

A. Main Program

Programs that perform multitasking must have TASK specified as an option in the PROC statement for the main program as follows:

name: PROC OPTIONS(MAIN,TASK);

B. Invoking Tasks

Tasks are initiated by subroutine calls. A task call differs from a subroutine call in that the task is not executed in sequence before control is returned to the calling program as with subroutines. Instead, processing continues in the calling program, and the task is executed concurrently. A relative priority can be set in the CALL statement to determine the priority with which the calling program and the task are to gain access to the computer's resources.

An *event-variable* is used to synchronize the invoking program with the task invoked by the call. The event-variable has two values associated with it; a completion code and a status code. The completion code is a bit-string with a value of '0'B for not complete and '1'B for complete. The status code is a binary fixed-point number with a value of zero indicating normal status.

1. CALL statement. The CALL statement is written as follows to invoke a task.

CALL *task(arguments)* TASK EVENT(*event-variable*) PRIORITY(*relative-priority*);

The TASK key word notifies the system that a task is being invoked. The *event-variable* is any unique PL/I name, and it does not have to be declared. The CALL statement automatically sets the event-variable completion code to '0'B and the status code to zero. The *relative-priority* is an expression with values ranging from -234 to $+234$ on S/360/370. The relative-priority determines the relative priority of the task with respect to the invoking program, and if PRIORITY is omitted, it defaults to the priority of the invoking program.

CALL GETALL(A,B,C) TASK EVENT(T1) PRIORITY(−1);

This call invokes the task GETALL and passes three arguments: A, B, and C: T1 is the event-variable, and the priority of GETALL is one less than that of the invoking program.

2. COMPLETION, STATUS functions. The invoking program can test for the completion of a task in two ways, with the COMPLETION function, and with the WAIT statement. The STATUS function returns the status code. The COMPLETION function, written as COMPLETION(*event-variable*) returns a value of '0'B if the task is not complete, or '1'B if the task is complete. The STATUS function, written as STATUS(*event-variable*), returns the status code.

3. WAIT Statement. The WAIT statement causes execution of the program to be suspended until specified completion codes are set to '1'B by tasks. It is written as follows:

WAIT(*event-variable,event-variable,...*) (*number*);

The WAIT statement waits for one or more *event-variables* to be set to completion by the tasks. The *number* is an expression that specifies the number of event-variables that must be set to completion before processing can continue.

WAIT(T1) (1);

This statement causes the invoking program to be suspended until the task that was called with EVENT(T1) completes.

WAIT(T1,T2,T3) (2);

Two of the three tasks must complete before processing continues.

C.   Tasks

A task is coded as a normal subroutine. However, a RETURN or END statement does not return control to the calling program, but simply terminates the task. The completion code is set to '1' and the status code is set to zero.

1. EXIT statement. The EXIT statement is used for abnormal termination of a task. It also sets the completion code to '1'B, but sets the status code to 1. Tasks can themselves invoke other subtasks, and any such subtasks are terminated when the task that invoked them is terminated.

2. COMPLETION, STATUS pseudovariables. The COMPLETION and STATUS functions can also be used as pseudovariables on the left side of an assignment statement to set completion codes and status codes.

COMPLETION(T1) = '1'B;   (The completion code for event-variable T1 is set
                                                                              to '1'B)

STATUS(T1) = 10;   (The status code for event-variable T1 is set to 10)

D.   I/O Tasks

The READ, WRITE, and DISPLAY I/O statements can also be made tasks by appending the EVENT(*event-variable*) option to the statements. The event-variable completion code is set to '1'B when the I/O operation completes, and the completion code can be tested or a WAIT statement can be issued to determine when the I/O operation completes. The statements are written as follows:

READ FILE(*file-name*) INTO (*variable*) EVENT(*event-variable*);
WRITE FILE(*file-name*) FROM (*variable*) EVENT(*event-variable*);
DISPLAY(*message*) REPLY(*variable*) EVENT(*event-variable*);

E.   DELAY Statement

The DELAY statement suspends execution of the issuing program for a given number of milliseconds. It is coded as follows:

DELAY(*milliseconds*); (The *milliseconds*, units of 0.001 seconds, can be an expression.)

F. Example of Multitasking

The following example gives a simple illustration of multitasking. A main program invokes a task to issue a message to the operator and await a response while the main program continues execution. The task in turn invokes a subtask to prompt the operator if he does not respond within a given time.

```
EXAMPLE: PROC OPTIONS(MAIN,TASK);
            (Tasks must be specified in the option list of the main program.)
         DCL MESSAGE CHAR(50), ANS CHAR(100);
            (Storage is reserved for the operator message and his response.)
         MESSAGE = 'HEY YOU! WHERE IS MY JOB?';
            (The message is formed.)
         CALL OPERATOR(MESSAGE,ANS) TASK EVENT(ALL_DONE);
            (The task OPERATOR is invoked, and the message is passed as an argument.
            A second argument is also passed, into which the operator's response is to
            be returned. ADD_DONE is used as the event-variable. Processing in the
            main program continues, and at some later point, the main program checks
            to see if the operator has responded.)
         IF COMPLETION(ALL_DONE) = '0'B
            (See if the operator has responded.)
            THEN DO;
               (If not, issue another message.)
               DISPLAY('HEY! I WANT MY JOB BACK.');
               WAIT(ALL_DONE) (1);
                  (Wait for the task to terminate.)
               END;
```

The OPERATOR task might be written as follows:

```
OPERATOR: PROC(MSG,ANS);
          DCL MSG CHAR(50), ANS CHAR(100);
          CALL RUDE TASK EVENT(RUDE_DONE);
             (A subtask named RUDE is invoked to prompt the operator every three
             seconds. RUDE_DONE is the event-name.)
          DISPLAY(MSG) REPLY(ANS);
             (Display the message to the operator. Execution is suspended until his
             response is stored in ANS.)
          END OPERATOR;
             (The task is terminated, and this in turn terminates the subtask RUDE.)
```

The RUDE subtask is written as follows:

```
RUDE:   PROC;
 AGAIN: DELAY(3000);
           (Wait three seconds.)
        DISPLAY('COME ON, COME ON!');
           (Prompt the operator with a message.)
        GO TO AGAIN;
           (Go wait three more seconds and do it again.)
        END RUDE;
```

G. Exercise

1. A program contains the following inefficient loop.

```
LOOP: DO I = 1 TO L*2;
        DO J = 1 TO L*10;
        DO K = 1 TO L/10;
        A(I+1,J+1,K+1) = B(I+1,J+1,K+1)**(X*2/Z);
        A(I+1,J+1,K+1) = MAX(A(I+1,J+1,K+1),SQRT(7));
        END LOOP;
```

Assume that you wish to make the loop more efficient. Write a higher priority task named TIME to print out the values of I, J, and K each 100 milliseconds so that as you optimize the loop you can measure your progress. (Ignore the effect that multiprogramming may have on your timings.)

VI.   RECURSION

Recursion is the ability to invoke a procedure, and then invoke the same procedure again before returning from the procedure. This can occur when a procedure invokes itself, or when it invokes another procedure that invokes the first procedure.

Recursion is made possible by the dynamic storage allocation of PL/I in which storage is allocated each time a procedure is entered. If a procedure is entered again before returning from the procedure, all old values are pushed down in a list. (Storage allocation is described in Chapter 7.) Recursive procedures must have the RECURSIVE option specified in the PROC statement.

A.   Example of Recursion

In the following example, a function is written that computes the value of 2^n by computing $2*2^{n-1}$, and then calling itself to compute 2^{n-1}. The 2^{n-1} is then computed as $2*2^{n-2}$, and so on until n equals 1.

```
N2: PROC(N) RECURSIVE RETURNS(FIXED);
      DCL N FIXED;
      IF N = 1 THEN RETURN(2);
              ELSE RETURN(2*N2(N-1));
      END N2;
```

The statement A = N2(3); causes the following to occur.

1.   N2 is invoked from the main program, and storage is allocated for N = 3.
2.   The RETURN(2*N2(2)) invokes N2 again. Storage is allocated for N = 2, and N = 3 is pushed down in a list.
3.   The RETURN(2*N2(1)) invokes N2 again. Storage is allocated for N = 1, and N = 2 is pushed down in a list.
4.   The RETURN(2) from step 3 returns a value of 2 to step 2. N = 1 is deleted, and N = 2 pops up to become active.
5.   The RETURN(2*2) from step 2 returns a value of 4 to step 1. N = 2 is deleted, and N = 3 pops up to become active.
6.   The RETURN(2*4) from step 1 returns a value of 8. N = 3 is deleted.

There are more efficient ways to program the above problem, such as coding 2**N directly. There are many applications of recursion, but its inappropriate use, as in the example above, is inefficient and makes programs hard to understand.

B. Exercises

1. Write a recursive function named FACT to calculate n-factorial. $(n*(n-1)*(n-2)*...)$

2. Write a recursive function named DIGITS to return the sum of the digits to the left of the decimal point in a floating-point number. For example, DIGITS(22.45) yields 4 and DIGITS (105924.6) yields 21.

Appendix A

PL/I Character	As Written for 48-Character Set
:	..
;	,.
%	//
&	AND
|	OR
¬	NOT
<	LT
< =	LE
>	GT
> =	GE
¬<	NL
¬=	NE
¬>	NG
||	CAT
- >	PT

The 48-character set words (LE, CAT, etc.) must be preceded and followed by a blank. The following example illustrates the use of the 48-character set:

START: IF (A | B) & (C > = D) THEN GO TO FINISH;
START.. IF (A OR B) AND (C GE D) THEN GO TO FINISH,.

Appendix B

Word	Abbreviation
%ACTIVATE	%ACT
ALLOCATE	ALLOC†
ALLOCATION(X)	ALLOCN(X)†
AUTOMATIC	AUTO
BINARY	BIN
BUFFERED	BUF
CHARACTER(length)	CHAR(length)
COLUMN(w)	COL(w)
COMPLEX	CPLX
COMPLEX(a,b)	CPLX(a,b)
CONDITION	COND†
CONTROLLED	CTL
CONVERSION	CONV
&DEACTIVATE	%DEACT
DECIMAL	DEC
DECLARE	DCL
%DECLARE	%DCL
DEFINED	DEF
ENVIRONMENT	ENV
EXCLUSIVE	EXCL
EXTERNAL	EXT
FIXEDOVERFLOW	FOFL
GO TO	GOTO
%GO TO	%GOTO
INITIAL	INIT
INTERNAL	INT
IRREDUCIBLE	IRRED
NOCONVERSION	NOCONV
NOFIXEDOVERFLOW	NOFOFL
NOOVERFLOW	NOOFL
NOSTRINGRANGE	NOSTRG
NOSUBSCRIPTRANGE	NOSUBRG
NOUNDERFLOW	NOUFL
NOZERODIVIDE	NOZDIV
OVERFLOW	OFL
PICTURE	PIC
POINTER	PTR
POSITION(i)	POS(i)
PRECISION(x,p[,g])	PREC(x,p[,g])
PROCEDURE	PROC
%PROCEDURE	%PROC
REDUCIBLE	RED

† Not all compilers have this abbreviation.

SEQUENTIAL	SEQL
STRINGRANGE	STRG
SUBSCRIPTRANGE	SUBRG
STRINGSIZE	STRZ†
UNALIGNED	UNAL
UNBUFFERED	UNBUF
UNDEFINEDFILE(file-name)	UNDF(file-name)
UNDERFLOW	UFL
VARYING	VAR
ZERODIVIDE	ZDIV

Appendix C

S/360/370 permits FORTRAN to invoke PL/I subroutines and functions and PL/I to invoke FORTRAN subroutines and functions. This is done with the PL/I Interlanguage Facility provided by some PL/I compilers. It is generally more efficient if the main program is a PL/I program, as this enables PL/I to get control first and return control to the system upon termination to minimize the more extensive PL/I housekeeping. (PL/I cannot call a FORTRAN main program.)

PL/I and FORTRAN can share data in core storage by defining the storage with labeled common in FORTRAN and EXTERNAL storage in PL/I as described in Chapter 8. The name of a labeled common area can match the name of an EXTERNAL structure in PL/I, and the PL/I structure can then define the individual data names in the same order in which they appear in the labeled COMMON statement. Variables are allocated storage in the order in which they are listed in the COMMON statement and in the DCL statement, which enables the same physical core location to be addressed by both FORTRAN and PL/I. Chapters 4 and 5 describe the corresponding FORTRAN and PL/I data types.

The OPTIONS(FORTRAN) clause is used to inform PL/I that it is to interface with FORTRAN. This permits PL/I to intercept subroutine arguments and compensate for such things as multiple-dimension arrays that are stored in a different order in PL/I than in FORTRAN. To invoke a FORTRAN subroutine or function from PL/I, code the following on the ENTRY statement in the PL/I program.

> DCL FNSUB ENTRY(*parameter-descriptions*) OPTIONS(FORTRAN);
> CALL FNSUB(A);

To invoke a PL/I subroutine or function from FORTRAN, code the following on the PROC statement in the PL/I program.

PLSUB: PROC(*parameters*) OPTIONS(FORTRAN);

Appendix D

Every computer problem usually has several correct solutions, each one perhaps better than the others judged by a particular criterion. A solution may be tightly coded to be very efficient, but it may be complex, inflexible, and make the program difficult to debug and maintain. One thing is clear—any acceptable solution must give correct results. They must be correct merely with a set of test data, but with the wide range of values and unexpected data that may occur in real situations.

Chapter 2

1

FORMULA Wrong—too long.	FORMULA
TEXT	TEXT
STOP_AT Wrong—too long. Underscore not permitted.	STOP_AT
2HOT Wrong—first character not alpha.	2HOT Wrong—first character not alpha.
F – 111 Wrong—minus sign not permitted.	F – 111 Wrong—minus sign not permitted.
H24	H24
HUT_16 Wrong—underscore not permitted.	HUT_16
OH** Wrong—asterisk not permitted.	OH** Wrong—asterisk not permitted.
A	A
MEET_ME@4 Wrong—too long, improper characters.	MEET_ME@4
UP TO Wrong—blanks not permitted.	UP TO
NOT—HERE Wrong—too long, dash not permitted.	NOT – HERE Wrong—minus sign not permitted.

2

100	100: Wrong—first character not alpha.
1	1: Wrong—first character not alpha.
10.7 Wrong—decimal point not permitted.	NOW Wrong—no colon.
1,000 Wrong—comma not permitted.	HERE:
100000 Wrong—too large.	TO_HERE:
1 1 Wrong—blank not permitted.	HERE: AND_HERE:
4725	EITHER/OR: Wrong—slash not permitted.
	ALL DONE: Wrong—blank not permitted.
	FINISH; Wrong—no colon.

3

Main program:

FORTRAN	PL/I
STOP	MAIN: PROC OPTIONS(MAIN);
END	END MAIN;

Subroutine:

SUBROUTINE SUB	SUB: PROC;
RETURN	END SUB;
END	

Function:

FUNCTION NAME	NAME: PROC;
NAME = 0	RETURN(0);
RETURN	END NAME;
END	

4

C MAIN PROGRAM   /* MAIN PROGRAM

                                                 No terminating */.

100	A = 100**2 − 7.6	100: A = 100**2 − 7.6 Bad label.
	+ 3.4 No continuation.	+ 3.4;
50	B = A/2.0	S50: B = A/2.0 Does not end with semicolon.

	IF(B.EQ.0)GOTO200	IF(B=0)THENGOTODONE;
	C = A*B C FIND A*B.	C = A*B /*FIND A*B*/;
	Comment must be on separate card.	
	GO TO 50	GO TO S50;
200	A = 0	DONE A = 0; No colon for label.
	END	END;

Chapter 3

1

A = 3., B = 2.	A = 4, B = 4

2

((A**B) − (2/Y)) − D	((A**B) − (2/Y)) − D
(A + ((2*(C**2))/B)) + (6*4)	(A + ((2*(C**2))/B)) + (6*4)
((A + B).EQ.0).OR.	((A + B) = 0) | ((A ¬= 1.0) &
((A.NE.1.0).AND.	(B > A))
(B.GT.A))	

3

IF (I.EQ.1) GO TO 600	IF I = 1 THEN GO TO S600;
IF (I − 3) 400,150,1000	ELSE IF I = 2 THEN GO TO S400;
	ELSE IF I = 3 THEN GO TO S150;

FORTRAN	PL/I

```
                                       ELSE IF I = 4 THEN GO TO
                                                           S1000;
        GO TO (600,400,150,1000),I     DCL LBL(4) INIT(S600,S400,S150,
                                                           S1000);
                                       GO TO LBL(I);
```

4

```
        IF (A.EQ.0.) J = 0             IF A = 0 THEN J = 0;
        IF ((A.LT.0.).AND.               ELSE IF (A < 0) & (B < = 0)
                (B.LE.0.)) J = −1                   THEN J = −1;
        IF ((A.GT.22.).AND.((B+C).     ELSE IF (A > 22) & ((B+C) > 22)
                GT.22.)) J = −2                     THEN J = −2;
        IF ((A.EQ.1.).OR.(B.EQ.1.).    ELSE IF (A = 1) | (B = 1) |
                OR.(((B+C)/2.).EQ.1.))    (((A+B)/2) = 1) THEN J = 100;
                J = 100
```

5

(a) −10, −7, −4, −1, 2, 5, 8, 11, 14, 17, 20, 23	−10, −7, −4, −1, 2, 5, 8, 11, 14, 17, 20
(b) 1	None
(c) —	−3, −5, −7, 8, 11, 16, 9, 7
(d) 1, 2, 3, 4	1, 2, 3

6

```
        DO 400 I = −3, −7, −1          DO I = −3 TO −7 BY −1;
                Negative increment
        IF (A(I).EQ.0.) GO TO 500      IF A(I) = 0 THEN GO TO S500;
        DO 400 J = 3,7                 DO J = 3 TO 7;
        IF (B(J).EQ.0.) GO TO 600      IF B(J) = 0 THEN GO TO S600;
                Cannot branch into middle         Cannot branch into middle of DO
                of DO loop.                        loop.
400     CONTINUE                       END; END;
500     J1 = I                         S500: J1 = I;
        DO 700 J = J1,100,10             DO J = J1 TO 100 BY 10;
600     B(J) = 100.                    S600: B(J) = 100;
700     IF (A(I).EQ.7.) GO TO 800      2700: IF A(I) = 7 THEN GO TO S800;
                Cannot end DO loop with
                IF statement.
800     CONTINUE                       END; S800:
```

7

```
        IDY = IDY + IDUR               IDY = IDY + IDUR;
100     IF (IDY.LE.30) GO TO 200       S100: IF IDY > 30
        IDY = IDY − 30                     THEN DO;
        IMO = IMO + 1                          IDY = IDY − 30;
        IF (IMO.LE.12) GO TO 100               IMO = IMO + 1;
        IYR = IYR + 1                          IF IMO > 12
```

FORTRAN:

```
            IMO = 1
            GO TO 100
200         CONTINUE
```

PL/I:

```
            THEN DO;
                IYR = IYR + 1;
                IMO = 1;
            END;
        GO TO S100;
        END;
```

8

FORTRAN:

```
            IDUR = (IYR2 − IYR1)*360
                + (IMO2 − IMO1)*30
                    +(IDY2 − IDY1)
```

PL/I:

```
            IDUR = (IYR2 − IYR1)*360
                        + (IMO2 − IMO1)*30
                            + (IDY2 − IDY1);
```

9

FORTRAN:

```
            TOTAL = 0.
            DO 100 I = 2, 50, 2
                IF (TOTAL.GT.1000.) GO
                                TO 300
100         TOTAL = TOTAL
                        + AMOUNT(I)
            DO 200 I = 51, 100, 3
                IF (TOTAL.GT.1000.) GO
                                TO 300
200         TOTAL = TOTAL
                        + AMOUNT(I)
300         CONTINUE
```

PL/I:

```
            TOTAL = 0;
            DO I = 2 TO 50 BY 2, 51 TO 100
                        BY 3 WHILE (TOTAL < =
                                    1000E0);
            TOTAL = TOTAL + AMOUNT(I);

            END;
```

10

FORTRAN:

```
            X = −6.
100         Y = (X − 1.0)/(X**2 + 1.0)
            X = X + .5
            IF (X.LE.10.) GO TO 100
```

PL/I:

```
            DO X = −6 TO 10 BY .5;
            Y = (X − 1)/(X**2 + 1);
            END;
```

Chapter 4

1

FORTRAN:

2	Integer.
22E7	Floating-point.
7.6	Floating-point.
(7.,2.)	Complex.
−9725.	Floating-point.
2D4	Double-precision floating-point.

PL/I:

2	Decimal fixed-point.
22E7	Floating-point.
7.6	Decimal fixed-point.
$7+2I$	Complex decimal fixed-point.
−9725.	Decimal fixed-point.
2E4	Floating-point.

2

FORTRAN:

A contains (1.,2.)
B contains 1.
C contains 2.

PL/I:

A contains $1E0 + 2E0I$
B contains 1E0
C contains 2E0

D contains (2.,3.)

D contains 2E0 + 3E0I

E contains (22749.,0.)

E contains 22749E0 + 0E0I

3

Decimal fixed-point:

DCL (FORCE, MASS, ACCEL)
FIXED DEC(12,5);

Integer:

INTEGER FORCE, MASS,
ACCEL

DCL (FORCE, MASS, ACCEL)
FIXED BIN(31);

Floating-point: (No declarations actually needed as variables will default properly.)

REAL FORCE, MASS,
ACCEL

DCL (FORCE, MASS, ACCEL)
FLOAT;

Double-precision floating-point:

REAL*8 FORCE, MASS,
ACCEL
or
DOUBLE PRECISION
FORCE, MASS, ACCEL

DCL (FORCE, MASS, ACCEL)
FLOAT(16);

Chapter 5

1

LOGICAL YES/.TRUE./,
NO/.FALSE./

DCL YES BIT(1) INIT('1'B),
NO BIT(1) INIT('0'B);

2

CH(1) = '1234', CH(2) = 'ZZbb',
L = 'ZZbb', M(1) = '9bbb',
M(2) = '4321',
M(3) = '4321'

CH(1) = 'XXXb', CH(2) = 'XXXb',
CH(3) = '1234'

3

```
         INTEGER ABCD/
         4HABCD/, DCBA/4HDCBA/
         ICT = 0
         DO 100 I = 1, 100
         IF (NAME.EQ.ABCD)
                 ICT = ICT + 1
         IF (NAME.EQ.DCBA)
                 ICT = ICT + 1
100      CONTINUE
```

```
ICT = 0;
DO I = 1 TO 100;
IF (NAME = 'ABCD') | (NAME =
    'DCBA') THEN ICT = ICT + 1;
END;
```

4

FORTRAN	PL/I

LOGICAL HOLIDY, RAIN,
                    WINDY, DAY
	DCL (HOLIDY, RAIN, WINDY,
	                              DAY) BIT(1);

INTEGER MONEY	DCL MONEY FIXED BIN(31);
REAL TEMP	DCL TEMP FLOAT;
DAY = .FALSE.	IF HOLIDY & ((¬ RAIN)&WINDY)
IF (HOLIDY.AND.((.NOT.	&(MONEY > 100)&((TEMP > 70)
C RAIN).AND.WINDY).	&(TEMP < 85))
C AND.(MONEY.GT.100).	THEN DAY = '1'B;
C AND.((TEMP.GT.70.0).	ELSE DAY = '0'B;
C AND.(TEMP.LT.85.0)))	
C DAY = .TRUE.	

5

Transfer is made to statement 100 for all values except IA = 0 and IS = 2.

6

DCL FLAG BIT(1);
FLAG = UNSPEC(SUBSTR(REC,
                    1,1)) = '11111111'B;

7

A contains HAZX'X and B contains '111101'

Chapter 6

1

FORTRAN	PL/I
I = 4	I = 4
A = 4.41889	A = 4.41889
J = 18	J = 18
B = −1.0	B = 0.166666
	C = 'Zbbbbb'
	D = '10'B

2

FORTRAN	PL/I

DOUBLE PRECISION
              ANS,A,B,C,W,X,Y,Z
	DCL (ANS,A,B,C,W,X,Y,Z)
	                              FLOAT(16);

ANS = ((A**(C/4D0) +
          B/3D0)*(Y + 2D0*
          X))/(B*A − W/Z)**
                    (N−1)
	DCL TWO FLOAT(16) INIT(2),
	          THREE FLOAT(16) INIT(3),
	          FOUR FLOAT(16) INIT(4);
	ANS = ((A**(C/FOUR) + B/
	          THREE)*(Y + TWO*X))/
	          (B*A − W/Z)**(N−1);

3

FORTRAN	PL/I

DOUBLE PRECISION
          FUTURE, INVEST, I
	DCL (FUTURE, INVEST, I)
	                              FIXED(12,2);

```
                I = 7.25D0                 I = 7.25;
                N = 10                     N = 10;
                INVEST = 100D0             DO INVEST = 100 TO 102 BY .05;
100             FUTURE = INVEST*           FUTURE = INVEST*((1 +
                    ((1D0 + I/100D0)**N)                    I/100)**N);
                INVEST = INVEST +          END;
                             .05D0
                IF (INVEST.LE.102D0)
                             GO TO 100
```

Chapter 7

1

```
                REAL SIZE(100)             DCL SIZE(100) FLOAT;
                DO 100 I = 1, 100          DO I = 1 TO 100;
100             SIZE(I) = I                SIZE(I) = I;
                                           END;
```

2

```
                IMPLICIT INTEGER           DCL (W,WAY,XERO) FIXED
                    (W−Z), REAL(K,N)                        DEC(9,5);
                LOGICAL TAX, FIRST,        DCL (TAX. FIRST, ONLY)
                             ONLY                          CHAR(115) VAR;
                DOUBLE PRECISION           DCL (KLEIN, NOT, IT) FLOAT;
                    KOST, WEIGHT, ZERO
                COMPLEX AREA, YOST         DCL (KOST, WEIGHT, ZERO)
                                                          FLOAT(16);
                                           DCL (AREA, YOST) COMPLEX;
```

3

```
                INTEGER SIZE(50,30,3,10)   DCL SIZE(50,30,3,10) FIXED
                                                           BIN(31);
                (45,000 elements)          (45,000 elements)
                TOTAL = 0.                 TOTAL = 0;
                DO 100 I = 1,50      LOOP: DO I = 1 TO 50;
                DO 100 J = 1,30            DO J = 1 TO 30;
                DO 100 K = 1,3            DO K = 1 TO 3;
                DO 100 L = 1,10           DO L = 1 TO 10;
100             TOTAL = TOTAL +           TOTAL = TOTAL +
                           SIZE(I,J,K,L)                SIZE(I,J,K,L);
                                           END LOOP;
```

4

```
        A(1,1) = 7                 A(1,1) = 3
        A(2,1) = 2                 A(1,2) = 3
        A(3,1) = 3                 A(2,1) = 2
        A(4,1) = 3                 A(2,2) = 7
        A(5,1) = 5                 A(3,1) = 2
```

FORTRAN	PL/I

A(1,2) = 2   A(3,2) = 2
A(2,2) = 2   A(4,1) is undefined
A(3,2) to A(5,2) are undefined.   A(4,2) is undefined
A(5,1) = 5
A(5,2) is undefined

5

```
INTEGER SIZE(1000,20)          DCL SIZE(1000,20) FIXED BIN(31),
REAL MAX(500,20)               MAX(500,20) FLOAT DEF SIZE;
EQUIVALENCE (SIZE(1,1),        As controlled storage:
           MAX(1,1))
                               DCL SIZE(1000,20) CTL FIXED
                                 BIN(31), MAX(500,20) CTL FLOAT;
                               ALLOCATE SIZE;
                               FREE SIZE;
                               ALLOCATE MAX;
                               FREE MAX;
```

6

```
DO 100 I = 1,99                LOOP: DO I = 1 TO 99;
K = I + 1                           DO J = I+1 TO 100;
DO 100 J = K, 100                   IF IVAL(J) < IVAL(I)
IF (IVAL(J).GE.IVAL(I))               THEN DO;
           GO TO 100
L = IVAL(J)                             L = IVAL(J);
IVAL(J) = IVAL(I)                       IVAL(J) = IVAL(I);
IVAL(I) = L                             IVAL(I) = L;
100    CONTINUE                         END;
                                    END LOOP;
```

7

```
DOUBLE PRECISION               DCL (XTRA, INT, TOTAL)
       XTRA, INT, TOTAL                      FLOAT(16) EXT;
INTEGER MAX(100,50)            DCL MAX(100,50) FIXED BIN(31)
                                                       EXT;
COMMON XTRA, INT,
       TOTAL, MAX
```

8

```
DIMENSION CITY(90),            DCL CITY(90) FLOAT,
       TOWN(30),BERG(30),             TOWN(30) FLOAT DEF
           HAMLET(30)                        CITY(1SUB),
EQUIVALENCE (TOWN(1),                 BERG(30) FLOAT DEF
       CITY(1)), BERG(1),                    CITY(1SUB+30),
       CITY(31)), (HAMLET(1),         HAMLET(30) FLOAT DEF
           CITY(61))                         CITY(1SUB+60);
```

9

```
            BLOCK DATA                      DCL SIZE(100) EXT INIT CALL
                                                                SUBRT;
            INTEGER SIZE(100)/100*0/    SUBRT: PROC;
            COMMON /NAME/SIZE                   SIZE = 0;
            END                                 RETURN;
                                                END SUBRT;
```

10

```
            REAL ACCEL(50,20),              DCL (ACCEL, MASS) (50,20)
                        MASS(50,20)                             FLOAT,
            INTEGER FORCE(50,20)              FORCE(50,20) FIXED BIN(31);
            DO 100 I = 1, 50               FORCE = ACCEL*MASS;
            DO 100 J = 1, 20
100         FORCE(I,J) = ACCEL(I,J)*
                        MASS(I,J)
```

Chapter 8

1

```
            SUBROUTINE RECTNG           RECTNG: PROC(LENGTH, WIDTH,
            (LENGTH, WIDTH, AREA)                             AREA);
            REAL LENGTH                      DCL LENGTH FLOAT;
            AREA = LENGTH*WIDTH              AREA = LENGTH*WIDTH;
            RETURN                           RETURN;
            END                              END RECTNG;
            —
            CALL RECTNG(100.,               CALL RECTNG(100E0,50E0,A);
                        50.,A)
```

2

```
            FUNCTION AREA               AREA: PROC(LENGTH,WIDTH)
                    (LENGTH,WIDTH)                    RETURNS(FLOAT);
            REAL LENGTH                      DCL LENGTH FLOAT;
            AREA = LENGTH*WIDTH             RETURN(LENGTH*WIDTH);
            RETURN                           END AREA;
            END                              —
            —                               DCL AREA ENTRY(FLOAT,
            A = AREA(100.,50.)                               FLOAT);
                                            A = AREA(100,50);
```

3

```
            SUBROUTINE ARRAY(A,         ARRAY: PROC(A,I,J);
                            I,J)
            DIMENSION A(I,J)                 DCL (I,J) FIXED, A(I,J) FLOAT;
            DO 100 K = 1,I                   LOOP: DO K = 1 TO I;
            DO 100 L = 1,J                        DO L = 1 TO J;
```

FORTRAN	PL/I
100 A(K,L) = K*L RETURN END — CALL ARRAY(B,M,N)	A(K,L) = K*L; END LOOP; RETURN; END ARRAY; — CALL ARRAY(B,M,N);

4

FORTRAN	PL/I

REAL FUNCTION
      METER(INCH)
REAL INCH
METER = INCH*0.0254
RETURN
ENTRY FEET(FT)
METER = FT*0.3048
 	
RETURN
ENTRY YARDS(YD)
 	
METER = YD*0.9144
RETURN
ENTRY MILES(ML)
REAL ML
METER = ML*1609.35
RETURN
END
	METER: PROC(INCH)
	      RETURNS(REAL);
	DCL INCH REAL;
	RETURN(INCH*0.0254);
	FEET: ENTRY(FT) RETURNS(REAL);
	RETURN(FT*0.3048);
	YARDS: ENTRY(YD)
	      RETURNS(REAL);
	RETURN(YD*0.9144);
	MILES: ENTRY(ML)
	      RETURNS(REAL);
	DCL ML REAL;
	RETURN(ML*1609.35);
	END METER;

5

FORTRAN	PL/I

REAL FUNCTION
      MINI(A,N,M)
DIMENSION A(N,M)
 	
MINI = A(1,1)
DO 100 I = 1, N
DO 100 J = 1, M
IF (A(I,J).LT.MINI)
      MINI = A(I,J)
100   CONTINUE
RETURN
END
	MINI: PROC(A,N,M)
	      RETURNS(REAL);
	DCL (N,M) FIXED, A(N,M)
	      REAL;
	ANS = A(1,1);
	LOOP: DO I = 1 TO N;
	DO J = 1 TO M;
	IF A(I,J) < ANS
	
	THEN ANS = A(I,J);
	END LOOP;
	RETURN(ANS);
	END MINI;

6

FORTRAN	PL/I
SUBROUTINE SET(I,J,K) DIMENSION I(J,K) DO 100 L = 1, J DO 100 M = 1, K	SET: PROC(I,J,K); DCL (J,K) FIXED, I(J,K) FIXED BIN(31); LOOP: DO L = 1 TO J; DO M = 1 TO K;

	FORTRAN	PL/I

```
         IF (I(L,M).LT.0) I(L,M) =              IF I(L,M) < 0
                           −1
         IF (I(L,M).GT.0) I(L,M) = 1               THEN I(L,M) = −1;
100      CONTINUE                                  ELSE IF I(L,M) > 0
         RETURN                                         THEN I(L,M)
                                                              = 1;
         END                                    END LOOP;
                                                RETURN;
                                                END SET;
```

7

```
         FUNCTION TAX(I)               TAX: PROC(I) RETURNS(FLOAT);
         TAX = 100.                         RETURN(100E0);
         RETURN                             END TAX;
         END
```

Chapter 9

1

```
         I = J*(FLOAT(K)/L)            I = J*(FLOAT(K,6)/L);
```

2

```
         DO 100 I = 1,10               VAL = SQRT(VAL);
         DO 100 J = 1,20
100      VAL(10,20) = SQRT(VAL
                         (I,J))
```

3

```
         FUNCTION KOUNT(I)            KOUNT: PROC(I) RETURNS(FIXED
                                                       BIN(31));
         KOUNT = 0                          DCL (I,KOUNT) FIXED
                                                       BIN(31));
100      IF (I.EQ.0) RETURN                 KOUNT = 0;
         IF (MOD(IABS(I),10).EQ.1)    LOOP: IF I = 0 THEN RETURN
            KOUNT = KOUNT + 1                         (KOUNT);
                                            IF MOD(ABS(I),10) = 1
                                                  THEN KOUNT = KOUNT
                                                              + 1;
         I = I/10                           I = I/10;
         GO TO 100                          GO TO LOOP;
         END                                END KOUNT;
```

4

```
         Y = EXP(X)*COS(THETA/        Y = EXP(X)*COSD(THETA)/
                 57.2958)/SQRT(Z)                  SQRT(Z);
         X = ABS(Y/Z)*ALOG(W)         X = ABS(Y/Z)*ALOG(W);
```

5

```
         I = SIGN(AMOD(ABS            I = MOD(ABS(TOTAL),10E0)*
            (TOTAL),10.),TOTAL)                      SIGN(TOTAL);
         J = SIGN(AMOD(ABS            J = MOD(ABS(TOTAL*10E0),
            (TOTAL*10.),10.),TOTAL)           10E0)*SIGN(TOTAL);
```

6

```
                                   SWITCH: PROC(STRING) RETURNS
                                              (CHAR(1000) VAR);
                                   DCL STRING CHAR(1000) VAR;
                                   DCL A CHAR(1);
                                   A = SUBSTR(STRING,1,1);
                                   SUBSTR(STRING,1,1) = SUBSTR
                                      (STRING,1,LENGTH(STRING));
                                   SUBSTR(STRING,1,LENGTH
                                              (STRING)) = A;
                                   RETURN(STRING);
                                   END SWITCH;
```

Chapter 10

1

```
         WRITE (6,100) I              DCL F6 FILE;
100      FORMAT(A(4))                 OPEN FILE(F6) OUTPUT;
         REWIND 6                     PUT FILE(F6) EDIT (A) (A(4));
200      READ (6,100,END=300) I       CLOSE FILE(F6);
         GO TO 200                    OPEN FILE(F6) INPUT;
300      CONTINUE                     ON ENDFILE(F6) GO TO S300;
                                   S200: GET FILE(F6) EDIT (A) (A(4));
                                         GO TO S200;
                                   S300:
```

2

```
         DIMENSION I1(100),           DCL (I1,I2) (100), (A1,A2) (100),
            I2(100),A1(100),A2(100),     J1(100) CHAR(7), J2(100) CHAR(9);
            J1(2,100),J2(3,100)
         I = 0                        ON ENDFILE (SYSIN) GO TO
                                                          S500;
100      I = I + 1                    DO I = 1 TO 100;
         IF (I.LE.100) GO TO 300      GET EDIT (I1(I),I2(I),A1(I),A2(I),
         WRITE (6,200)                              J1(I),J2(I))
200      FORMAT(24H ERROR—             (COL(1),(2)(F(7),F(9)),A(7),A(9));
            TOO MANY RECORDS)
         STOP
300      READ (5,400,END=500)         END;
            I1(I),I2(I),A1(I),A2(I),J1(1,   PUT EDIT ('ERROR—TOO MANY
            I),J1(2,1),(J2(J,I),J=1,3)              RECORDS') (SKIP,A(23));
```

FORTRAN		PL/I

```
400        FORMAT(I7,I9,F7.0,F9.0,              STOP;
                A4,A3,2A4,A1)           S500: PUT EDIT (I−1,'RECORDS
           GO TO 100                              READ IN') (SKIP,F(3),A(16));
500        I = I−1
           WRITE (6,600) I
600        FORMAT(1H ,I3,16H
               RECORDS READ IN)

3
           NAMELIST/FIRST/TOTAL,               PUT DATA(TOTAL,SIZE,FORM,
               SIZE,FORM,DIST                              LIST);
           WRITE (6,FIRST)

4
           WRITE (6,100) LIST,LIST,            PUT EDIT(LIST,LIST,LIST,'bbb')
               LIST,LIST
100        FORMAT(T10,A1,T19,A2,                  (COL(10),A(1),COL(19),A(2),
               T19,X1,T28,A3,T28,X2,              COL(19),X(1),COL(28),A(3),
               T37,A4,T37,X3)                      COL(28),X(2),COL(37),A(4),
                                                   COL(37),A(3));

5
           DIMENSION IN(100,8),                DCL (IN,IM) (100,8), IT(8);
               IM(100,8)
           I = 0                               ON ENDFILE(SYSIN) GO TO
                                                               S300;
100        I = I + 1                           DO I = 1 TO 100;
           IF (I.GT.100) GO TO 300             GET EDIT(IN(I,J) DO J = 1 TO 8)
           READ (6,200,END=300)                              ((10)F(10));
               (IN(I,J),J=1,8)
200        FORMAT(8I10)                        END;
           GO TO 100                     S300: DO J = 1 TO I−1;
300        I = I − 1                             IT(*) = IN(J,*);
           DO 400 J = 1,I                        WRITE FILE(F9) FROM (IT);
400        WRITE (9) (IN(J,K),K=1,8)             END;
           REWIND 9                            CLOSE FILE(F9);
           DO 500 J = 1,I                       OPEN FILE(F9) INPUT;
           READ (9) (IM(J,K),K=1,8)       LOOP: DO J = 1 TO I−1;
           DO 500 K = 1,8                          READ FILE(F9) INTO (IT);
           IF (IM(J,K).NE.IN(J,K))                 DO K = 1 TO 8;
               WRITE (6,450)                       IF IM(J,K) ¬= IN(J,K)
450        FORMAT(20H ERROR—                      THEN PUT EDIT ('ERROR—
               DOESN'T MATCH)                        DOESN''T MATCH')
500        CONTINUE                                            A(20));
                                               END LOOP;

6
           IPAGE = 0                           ON ENDPAGE(SYSPRINT)
           DO 200 N = 1, 901, 100                  BEGIN;
```

FORTRAN	PL/I
``` IPAGE = IPAGE + 1 WRITE (6,100) IPAGE 100 FORMAT(1H1,26X, 21HTABLE OF SQUARE ROOTS, 20X, 4HPAGE, I4,//,1H ,6X,19HNUMBER SQUARE ROOT,16X, 19HNUMBER SQUARE ROOT,//) ```	``` PAGE = PAGE + 1; PUT EDIT ('TABLE OF SQUARE ROOTS', 'PAGE', PAGE,'NUMBER SQUARE ROOT', 'NUMBER SQUARE ROOT') (PAGE,X(26),A(21),X(20),A(4), F(4),SKIP(2),X(6),A(19),X(16), A(19)); PUT SKIP(2); END; ```

```
        NP = N + 49                   PAGE = 0;
        DO 200 NL = N, NP      LOOP: DO N = 1 TO 901 BY 100;
        NR = NL + 50                  SIGNAL
        A = NL                            ENDPAGE(SYSPRINT);
                                      DO NL = N TO N+49;
        AL = SQRT(A)                  PUT EDIT (NL,SQRT(NL),
        AR = SQRT(A + 50.)                NL + 50, SQRT(NL + 50))
200     WRITE (6,300) N,AL,NR,AR      (COL(1),F(10),F(14,5),X(11),F(10),
300     FORMAT(1H ,I10,F14.5,                             F(14,5));
              11X,I10,F14.5)          END LOOP;
```

8

FORTRAN	PL/I
``` DIMENSION FLOAT(30), FMT(6),A(2) DATA FMT/4H(F5.,2H0), 4H(F10,3H.2),4H(F5.,2H0)/ READ (5,100) I 100 FORMAT(I1) A(1) = FMT(I*2 − 1) A(2) = FMT(I*2) DO 200 J = 1,30 READ (5,A) FLOAT(J) 200 WRITE (6,300) FLOAT(J) 300 FORMAT(1H ,F10.2) ```	``` DCL FLOAT(30) FLOAT; GET EDIT (I) (COL(1),F(1)); DO J = 1 TO 30; GET EDIT(FLOAT(J)) (R(FMT(I))); PUT SKIP EDIT (FLOAT(J)) (R(FMT(I))); END; FMT(1): FORMAT(COL(1),F(5)); FMT(2): FORMAT(COL(1),F(10,2)); FMT(3): FORMAT(COL(1),F(4)); ```

9

FORTRAN	PL/I
``` DATA ICH/1HI DIMENSION IREC(380) IN = 0 IOUT = 0 IEXC = 0 100 READ (9,200,END=400) IREC 200 FORMAT(380A1) ```	``` DCL REC CHAR(380); REC_IN, REC_OUT, REC_EXC = 0; ON ENDFILE(IN) GO TO DONE; READ IN: READ FILE(IN) INTO (REC); REC_IN = REC_IN + 1; IF SUBSTR(REC,63,1) = 'I' THEN REC_EXC = REC_EXC + 1; ```

```
                    IN = IN + 1
                    IF (IREC(63).EQ.ICH)
                              GO TO 300
                    WRITE (10,200) IREC

                    IOUT = IOUT + 1
                    GO TO 100
300                 IEXC = IEXC + 1
                    GO TO 100
400                 WRITE (6,500) IN,IOUT,
                                        IEXC
500                 FORMAT(1H ,3I6)
```

```
                    ELSE DO;
                        WRITE FILE(OUT)
                                FROM (REC);
                        REC_OUT + REC_OUT
                                        + 1;
                    END;
                    GO TO READ_IN;
DONE: PUT DATA(REC_IN,
                    REC_OUT,REC_EXC);
```

Chapter 11

1

```
                    CALL OVERFLOW(I)
                    CALL DVCHK(J)
                    K = ((B**N)/D)*(I(L)*J)
                    CALL OVERFLOW(I)
                    CALL DVCHK(J)
                    WRITE (6,100) I,J
100                 FORMAT(1H ,2I3)
```

```
ON CONV PUT EDIT
    ('CONVERSION ERROR') (A(132));
ON FOFL PUT EDIT
        ('FIXED OVERFLOW ERROR')
                        (A(132));
ON OFL PUT EDIT ('OVERFLOW
            ERROR') (A(132));
ON UFL PUT EDIT
    ('UNDERFLOW ERROR') (A(132));
ON ZDIV PUT EDIT ('ZERO
            DIVIDE ERROR') (A(132));
ON SIZE PUT EDIT ('SIZE
            ERROR') (A(132));
ON SUBRG PUT EDIT
    ('SUBSCRIPT RANGE ERROR')
                        (A(132));
(SIZE,SUBRG): K = ((B**N)/D)*
                    (I(L)*J);
```

2

```
                    DIMENSION A(20)
                    I = 1
100                 READ (9,200,ERR = 300,
                            END = 400) A
200                 FORMAT(20A4)
                    I = I + 1
                    GO TO 100
300                 PAUSE I
                    GO TO 100
400                 I = I - 1
                    PAUSE I
```

```
DCL A CHAR(80), B CHAR(132);
I = 1;
ON ENDFILE(F9) GO TO DONE;

ON TRANSMIT(F9)
    DISPLAY('ERROR IN
        RECORD' ‖ I) REPLY(B);
READ_IN: READ FILE(F9) INTO (A);
    I = I + 1;
    GO TO READ IN;
DONE: DISPLAY('RECORDS
        READ:' ‖ I - 1);
```

3

```
                                    ON CONVERSION BEGIN;
                                    DCL A CHAR(1);
                                    A = ONCHAR;
                                    PUT DATA(A);
                                    ONCHAR = '0';
                                    END;
```

4

```
                                    ON ENDFILE(PAYROLL) PUT
                                        EDIT ('END-OF-FILE') (A(132));
                                    ON UNDF(PAYROLL) PUT EDIT
                                        ('UNDEFINED FILE') (A(132));
                                    ON RECORD(PAYROLL) PUT
                                            EDIT ('WRONG RECORD
                                                LENGTH') (A(132));
                                    ON TRANSMIT(PAYROLL) PUT
                                        EDIT ('I/O ERROR') (A(132));
```

5

```
                                    (CHECK(START,READ_MORE,
                                    ALL_DONE,SQRT,SUBSTR,
                                    MAX,VALUES)): (NOUFL,
                                    SUBRG):
                                    COMPUTE: PROC OPTIONS
                                                    (MAIN);
                                        ON SUBRG PUT EDIT
                                        ('ERROR IN SUBSCRIPT
                                                    SIZE') (A(132));
```

Chapter 12

Section I

1

    (a) All
    (b) None
    (c) TWO.P.C(1) is stored in ONE.A.C(1)
    (d) TWO.S is stored in ONE.G
    (e) TQO.P.D(1) ∥ TWO.P.Q(1) is stored in ONE.H

2

```
        DUP: PROC OPTIONS(MAIN);
                DCL 1 REC,
                        2 NO CHAR(4),
                        2 NAME CHAR(25),
                        2 PCT DEC(6,2);
```

```
              DCL SAVE LIKE REC;
              ON ENDFILE(IN) GO TO DONE;
              NDUP = 0;
              READ FILE(IN) INTO (SAVE);
GET_NEXT: READ FILE(IN) INTO (REC);
              IF REC.NO = SAVE.NO
                  THEN NDUP = NDUP + 1;
                  ELSE SAVE = REC;
              GO TO GET_NEXT;
DONE: PUT DATA(NDUP);
END DUP;
```

Section II

1

264.7	000.3
1264bb	b33424
/b**1/	/b110/
bbbbb$1.10CR	$10,429.64bb
$120,514.21	$bbbbb77.40
$b − 133.25	$bbb23.98
543023.4	082398.4

2

```
DCL 1 HDR1,
      2 SP            CHAR(1) INIT('1'),
      2 T1            CHAR(18) INIT('SQUARES OF NUMBERS'),
      2 T2            CHAR(12) INIT(' '),
      2 T3            CHAR(4) INIT ('PAGE'),
   2 PAGE            PIC 'ZZZ9' INIT(0);
DCL HDR2            CHAR(17) INIT('bNUMBERbbbb SQUARE');
DCL BLANK           CHAR(1) INIT(' ');
DCL 1 PRINT_LINE,
      2 SP            CHAR(1) INIT(' '),
      2 NO            PIC 'ZZZ9',
      2 S1            CHAR(6) INIT(' '),
      2 SQ            PIC 'Z,ZZZ,ZZ9':
ON RECORD(OUT);
LINE = 0;
DO N = 1 TO 1000;
IF LINE = 0
   THEN DO;
         PAGE = PAGE + 1;
         WRITE FILE(OUT) FROM (HDR1);
```

```
                    WRITE FILE(OUT) FROM(BLANK);
                    WRITE FILE(OUT) FROM(HDR2);
                    WRITE FILE(OUT) FROM(BLANK);
                    LINE = 50;
                    END;
          NO = N;
          SQ = N*N;
          WRITE FILE(OUT) FROM (PRINT LINE);
          LINE = LINE - 1;
          END;
```

Section III

1

```
          % DCL FLOAT CHAR;
          %FLOAT = 'FIXED BIN(31)';
```

2

```
          %DCL (SIZE,I,J) FIXED;
          %SIZE = 100;
          DCL MAX(SIZE) FIXED DEC(2) INIT(
             %J = 0;
             %DO I = 1 TO SIZE;
             %J = J + 1;
             %IF J > 10 %THEN %J = 1;
               J
             %IF I = SIZE %THEN %GO TO SKIP;

             %SKIP: END;
               );
```

3

```
          %SIZE: PROC(I,J) RETURNS (CHAR);
                 DCL (I,J,K) FIXED;
                 K = (I-1)*8 + J;
                 RETURN('SIZF(' || K || ')');
                 %END SIZE;
          %DCL SIZE ENTRY(FIXED, FIXED) RETURNS(CHAR);
```

4

```
          %DCL I FIXED;
          %DO I = 1 TO 10;
          V1(I) = V1(I)/W(11-I);
          V2(11-I) = V2(11-I)/W(I+10);
          %END;
```

Section IV

1

```
      DCL 1 FORM,
          2 FLAG CHAR(1),
          2 NUMBER CHAR(4),
          2 AMOUNT CHAR(4),
          2 TIME CHAR(4);
      DCL 1 FORM2 BASED (P1),
          2 FLAG CHAR(1),
          2 NUMBER FLOAT(6),
          2 AMOUNT FLOAT(6),
          2 TIME FLOAT(6);
      DCL 1 FORM3 BASED (P2),
          2 FLAG CHAR(1),
          2 NUMBER FIXED BIN(31),
          2 AMOUNT FIXED BIN(31),
          2 TIME FIXED BIN(31);
      P1, P2 = ADDR(FORM);
      ON ENDFILE(IN) GO TO DONE;
READ_MORE: READ FILE(IN) INTO (FORM);
       IF FORM.FLAG = '1'
          THEN PUT EDIT(FORM) (SKIP,A(1),(3)(X(2),A(4)));
          ELSE IF FORM.FLAG = '2'
                  THEN PUT EDIT(FORM2) (SKIP,A(1),(3)(X(2),F(13.6)));
                  ELSE PUT EDIT(FORM3) (SKIP,A(1),(3)(X(2),F(6)));
      GO TO READ_MORE;
DONE:
```

2

```
DCL (FIRST,LAST) POINTER;
DCL 1 NUMBER BASED (NEXT),
    2 VALUE FIXED,
    2 PTR POINTER;
/* STORE THE NUMBERS */
ALLOCATE NUMBER SET(FIRST);
VALUE = 1;
DO I = 2 TO 100;
LAST = NEXT;
ALLOCATE NUMBER;
VALUE = I;
PTR = NULL;
LAST - > PTR = NEXT;
END;
/* FREE THE NUMBERS */
DO WHILE (FIRST ¬= NULL);
NEXT = FIRST;
FIRST = PTR;
```

```
          FREE NUMBER:
          END;
```

Section V

1

```
PROGRAM: PROC OPTIONS(MAIN,TASK);
          CALL TIMER TASK EVENT(EVAR) PRIORITY(1);
          LOOP: DO I = 1 TO L*2;
                    ⋮
                    END LOOP;
TIMER: PROC;
        DCL MSG CHAR(16) INIT('100 MILLISECONDS');
        PAUSE: DELAY(100);
                PUT DATA(MSG,I,J,K);
                GO TO PAUSE;
      END TIMER;
      END PROGRAM;
```

Section VI

1

```
FACT: PROC(N) RECURSIVE RETURNS(FIXED);
      DCL N FIXED;
      IF N = 1 THEN RETURN(1);
              ELSE RETURN(N*FACT(N – 1));
      END FACT;
```

2

```
DIGITS: PROC(NO) RECURSIVE RETURNS(FIXED);
          DCL NO FLOAT, I FIXED;
          IF ABS(NO < 1E0 THEN RETURN(0);
                      ELSE DO;
                              I = MOD(ABS(NO),10E0);
                              NO = NO/10E0;
                              RETURN(I + DIGITS(NO));
                              END;
      END DIGITS;
```

Index